The Voice Book

THE VOICE BOOK

*For actors, public speakers,
and everyone who wants to
make the most of their voice*

Michael McCallion

THEATRE ARTS BOOKS/ROUTLEDGE
NEW YORK

First published in the United States of America in 1988
by Theatre Arts Books/Routledge
29 West 35 Street
New York, New York 10001

Printed in Great Britain by
Mackays of Chatham Ltd, Kent
All rights reserved

U.S. Library of Congress
Cataloging in Publication Data
available.

To Anna, who knows the work best
and found the best way to get me to write about it,
and to Hugh, who gave me the chance to practise it
and so discover it,
this book is dedicated with love
and respect.

Contents

SPEECH

List of Illustrations

Complete List of Exercises

Foreword

In 1979 I was invited by the Society of Teachers of the Alexander
Technique to give the annual F. Matthias Alexander Memorial
Lecture. The theme was to be the relationship between the Alexander
Technique and my work with professional actors and students at
the Royal Academy of Dramatic Art. When I came to write up my
lecture notes for publication I was dissatisfied with the result and
saw that to do the subject justice a short book was required. But
the book might never have appeared were it not for the final push
which came from José-Luis Gómez, then Director of the Teatro
Nacional Español, when I was working with his company in Madrid
in 1982. He asked for a simplified written version of the work I had
been doing with the company. This I duly produced. Expanded into
an attempt to answer most of the questions which professional
voice users ask about the voice, here is the book. It is a practical
manual for voice users of all kinds.

My thanks then are due, first to Walter Carrington and the
members of the Society of Teachers of the Alexander Technique, to
my students and fellow actors, to José-Luis Gómez and the company
of the Teatro Nacional Español, and also to the British Council for
its support of my work in Spain, Portugal, Chile and Turkey while
I was writing this book. My thanks are also due to those patient
friends and colleagues here and in the USA who read the manuscript
and made many invaluable suggestions – and above all to my wife
Anna.

MM
Madrid 1982
Mastrouby 1984

Introduction

The processes of voice and speech are tested more thoroughly in the theatre than anywhere else and so this book addresses itself primarily to actors, drama students and singers. But the method of work it describes, particularly with regard to the mechanics of voice production, is being used effectively not only by actors and opera singers but also by lawyers and preachers, auctioneers and teachers; it's helpful to pop singers, politicians and businessmen. All kinds of people, for all sorts of reasons, are dissatisfied with the sound of their voice. Sometimes this is a question of accent, more often it's because they feel the voice itself could be a better means of self-expression if only they knew how to use it. Usually they are right. With this in mind, I have designed the book so that anyone without specialist knowledge can follow the work process and make the best use of one of our most important means of communication. So, this book is for anyone who wishes to use his or her voice well.

Using your voice well means three things:

1 You should be able to produce your voice without ever hurting yourself in the process.

2 You should be able to use your voice fully and energetically for several hours a day and have it as free and flexible at the end of your day's work as at the beginning.

3 Your voice must be capable of conveying all the nuances of meaning your work demands; it must be a completely flexible and accurate instrument of expression and communication which remains absolutely under your control.

The voice is an expression of what is going on mentally and physically in the speaker. It follows that we must find a way of training the mental and physical processes involved so that we produce in our voice and speech what we really choose to produce, so that we communicate what we wish to communicate.

Most of the things which go wrong with the voice do not begin with the vocal organs. It is a basic premiss of this book that most people actively interfere with the way their voices should work, and that interference begins with the way they use the body as a whole. If we can stop that interference the voice will work well.

That is why the first section of the book doesn't concern itself directly with voice but with body use, and too, why the exercises are kept to a minimum. The task is to get the voice functioning really efficiently all the time as part of a larger efficiency in the use of the whole body so that the heightened demands of playing a role, preaching a sermon or addressing a meeting can be easily met because no fundamental change of voice use is called for.

The way we live and the way we use our voice in our daily life is our basic exercise.

Nevertheless you will still need to find time, particularly at the beginning, to focus your energies on specific problems and deal with them. So you will find in each section of the book special exercises for special problems, and general exercises to develop skills – and muscles.

Not everyone can work with a good voice teacher and this book sets out to show you how to do the job of making the most of your voice by yourself. If you liberate the functioning of your voice, you will find you enjoy using it and will want to explore ways of doing so. My concern has been to point out and explain the means whereby you can help yourself to do what you want with your voice within the necessary and structural limitations that nature imposes – and to help you get rid of the limitations which are not necessary.

An Explanation
of the Form of the Book

———

The five sections of the book, Body Use, Breathing, Tuning, Speech, and Using Your Voice make a progression. When the body work is right the breathing mechanism is set free to function properly; in turn, this supports the vocal mechanism while air is tuned and resonated as voice in the process of phonation; then the tuned airflow is shaped into speech, and how that is done can affect the voice quality. These are all mechanical or physical processes and their functioning can be helped or hindered by the way we use them for communication; it's quite possible for someone to have mastered the physical processes of voice production and still find that the urgency or nervousness brought about by the need to use the voice in public undoes all the preparatory work. So in the last section of the book we look at the practical applications of voice use in the theatre, the studio or wherever your work calls for extraordinary skill in vocal communication.

Explanations of the phonetic symbols used in this book will be found in the Tables starting on p. 133.

BODY USE

The voice as an expression of the whole person

The most important physical elements in voice production (breathing, phonation and articulation) are all processes which occur because of the response of muscles to nervous stimulation, so in a sense, all of this book is about body use.

You cannot separate your voice use from the rest of you. The impulse to communicate vocally comes from and uses your whole person, not merely the vocal organs. And your whole person is affected in a mechanical or physical way by such things as your environment, your relationship with yourself and other people and your intention of the moment. And however your mechanical use is affected, so is your voice, which is an expression of yourself and what all of that self is doing.

So it is worthwhile thinking about what you do with your body before you begin to work on your voice, because for good or ill, that is the foundation upon which your voice use rests.

Babies and football fans

Babies can scream for hours and not hurt themselves or lose their voices. On the other hand, a visit to a football match will often leave a burly man with a worn-out laryngitic croak of a voice. Why should the baby be more efficient about making a loud noise than the football fan?

The baby, in response to whatever stimulus is provoking it to yell, just does it. Because the baby hasn't learned to get in the way of its own efficient functioning, it uses its body in the way it was designed to be used. The results may be torture for those around, but they don't hurt the baby.

The football fan's vocal mechanism is no less efficiently designed than the baby's, and he should be able to support his home team for a couple of hours without losing his voice. If he can't it's because he is doing or has done something to *interfere* with the functioning of his voice.

Baby and football fan are *using* their bodies; we may say that the baby has GOOD USE, but the croaking football fan has somehow acquired MISUSE.

Misuse

Where does this misuse in the football fan come from? Why does he interfere with a mechanism (his voice) which if left alone to get on with the job would do it perfectly well?

He has lived a lot longer than the baby. All of that living time he has been learning, and choosing how to adapt himself so that he can feel reasonably well adjusted to cope with the pattern of his life. His moment-by-moment responses to the daily business of living may have served him well – at that moment. But perhaps in the long term their effects may turn out to have been rather less than helpful, from a physical point of view, even perverse. It doesn't make much sense in the face of the evidence to smoke, but for some it is the chosen way of getting through the day without breaking down. Perhaps the smoking began as a casual indulgence, or a way of being sociable; eventually it became a habit and a prop and then an addiction. So what started as a choice eventually led to behaviour where choice played little or no part and an automatic need had replaced choice. As with smoking, so with other physical happenings. And some of the habits of use we acquire may stop us from making efficient physical responses to quite ordinary stimuli.

Of course another consideration in the case of the football fan is that he may be trying to do the impossible and shout louder than all of the other forty thousand fans put together! The impossible remains the impossible – we can only go to the limits which nature has imposed, and although those limits often allow us vastly more scope for action than we suppose, they are, nevertheless, limits.

But as for the limits which we rather than nature have imposed, they can be acquired in many ways and for many reasons. Let us consider three cases.

The case of the quiet monk

A monk came to me just after he had been given the task of running a parish. This involved him in a great deal of public speaking, sermon giving and some teaching. He wanted lessons because he kept losing his voice. Up to the time when he became a parish priest he had lived in the monastery, where he sang the divine office every day and said Mass, but otherwise seems to have spent very little time talking. His environment was quiet and quietly he lived in it for several years. When he came to see me he talked quietly and at that moment suffered no voice strain, although he did seem to need a breath more frequently than most people. Perhaps this was because there was very little movement in his rib-cage – far less than would be normal; also there was very little tonus in his abdominal muscles and his back was clearly weak. To find out what else was going on I went to see him preach. At the moment he began it was obvious he was fighting for breath and was certainly striving very hard to make himself heard. His striving took the form of throwing his head back as he gasped for air and violently lifting his whole rib-cage as the air went in; then with equal violence he pushed the rib-cage down again as he began to speak; there was a great whoosh of air on the first syllable or two and then he was fighting for breath again. In this way, by trying to make good his vocal deficiencies he was doing just about everything he could to make matters worse.

After discussing the problem, we came to the conclusion that a life of quiet study and contemplation had produced two effects: a deterioration of the muscles responsible for supporting the voice, and a consequent fear of having to produce the voice fully. I asked him if he could remember what his voice had been like before he became a monk; he laughed, quietly, and said he had had a very loud voice which had caused him some embarrassment when he joined the order. At an early stage he had been reprimanded for singing too loudly in choir. Thereafter it had been a point of obedience with him to make as little noise as possible. He had succeeded only too well. For twenty or so years he had, from a vocal point of view, been deconditioning his body. Now he found it a mental and physical fight to produce enough voice to fill the parish church. We might say that in the case of the quiet monk, the environmental pressures produced habits of use which were too much for his voice to cope with.

The case of the timid actor

The actor in question was young and gifted but shy. At the point of his training when I met him he had only two modes of expression: his everyday behaviour was quiet and withdrawn, but when he acted a monstrous change came over him; the veins in his throat stood out like hawsers, he was tense from head to foot and he lost his voice during the course of the performance. The fight which was going on in him to break the barriers of his shyness and justify his presence on a stage produced several effects. In his everyday use he tended to drop his chin, collapse his neck and hunch his shoulders forward; but when he was acting he felt this use to be inadequate and so he did something different: he pushed his head forward and pulled his shoulders up and back; but his throat was as blocked as in his everyday use and he had to force the breath in the process of vocalizing. The extraordinary tensions this produced in the throat, abdominal muscles and back, together with associated tensions in his legs, made him quite uncontrolled in his acting: he shouted (until voice loss set in) rather than talked, and all his movements were violent and lacking in co-ordination. At this time his process of self-correction was useless because it didn't take into account the basic effects his shyness had had on his body use: a non-functioning in the head/neck/back relationship; his neck was still collapsed even when he pushed his head forward. Later he was able to correct this, and although still shy as a private person, though perhaps less so, he no longer found it necessary to produce a massive over-compensation on the stage. He had altered his basic use. His acting was still energetic, but now, focused and communicative and used as he wanted to use it. His energy served his acting intentions instead of getting in the way.

The case of the shot barrister

This case was interesting to me at the time because the barrister in question had suffered such massive physical damage that I doubted voice classes would do much good. The barrister shared my pessimism. However, both of us were bullied into action by his wife. In the 1939–45 war the barrister had been shot. The bullet had passed through a variety of abdominal muscles, through the diaphragm, upwards through a lung and had finally left his body through the wall of the chest near his shoulder blade. The shot lung was removed in the field hospital, so some of this physical damage was irreversible. The point of the classes was to try to achieve some kind of voice: when he came, the barrister spoke in a series of hisses. Eventually we found that some measure of vocal control could be re-established and the barrister could resume his advocacy without sounding like an enraged snake. The point was this: the wound had been severe and so was the reaction. In order to avoid pain, the barrister had chosen to limit the action of his rib-cage and diaphragm. This made him feel inadequately supported for full normal vocalization, so he whispered. In fact this use of breath was most inefficient; less breath is used, proportionately, when the voice is well-tuned than when the air is passed through the glottis untuned. Also, although the pain from his wound had ceased some twenty-five years before, the barrister had still hung on to his compensatory use, and as a result it had become habitual. Undoing the habitual response produced a good and serviceable voice. Both of us had been wrong at first in supposing that nothing could mend the situation – his wife had had more sense.

Change and choice

In the three examples just given, established patterns of use turned out to be quite changeable. Both the actor and the barrister were of the opinion that what they did with their bodies was an inevitable part of being themselves. This wasn't so. A large number of people entertain similar misconceptions.

What we are is to a large extent what we make ourselves. Having made ourselves one pattern of use, we can unmake it, or make another. It's a question of choice and of knowing how to go about it.

Part of our survival equipment as human beings is mobility, something we share with most animals. Because we move a lot, we need to be protected as we do so, so that we don't damage ourselves. Our chief means of protection during mobility are the postural mechanisms which keep us balanced. As we learn to stand, walk, run and jump, these postural mechanisms develop so that we don't have to work out how to do our moving. When we slip on a banana skin we perform prodigies of rapid adjustment in our balance to stop our heads coming into violent contact with the planet. There's no time in mid-skid to work out consciously what we need to do to save the brain-case from injury, so our reactions, the interplay of the many different muscular tensions involved, are likely to be subconscious and involuntary. We perform most of our movements in the same way: we may be conscious that we want to lift a cup to take a drink, or we want to speak; we are not conscious of how we do these actions.

If all of our moving and living were on this subconscious or involuntary basis we'd probably always be making the best use of our bodies – and our voices. But we also have a highly developed consciousness, and that brings with it the possibility of choice. The choices we make to ease a short-term or local difficulty may, by dint of repetition, become habit, and so part of our subconscious behaviour and no longer operate from choice. If the original choices were good (from the point of view of keeping the body working well) then there is no problem. But if the original choices, now fossilized as habit, lead to an inefficient functioning in the long term, then we face an interlock of related problems if we want to restore efficient functioning.

The first problem is that because what we do is habitual, it feels right, and so is difficult to detect as a wrong except in the end result it is producing – a sore throat when we speak loudly perhaps, or backache after sitting at a typewriter for several hours. The second problem is that our habitual responses are part of the behavioural pattern by which we know our self, and we're always loath to interfere with whatever our established sense of self is: perhaps if we do that we won't any longer be that self, and then where are we? Who are we? This is a problem which often deters people from making changes in their voice use, because any radical change of voice use feels so false to the sense of self. It's a question of self-misrepresentation, or perhaps misconception: the self will remain secure even while we change many of its uses.

But if we are to change the fossilized and involuntary response, we have to use consciousness to do it. We have to know what it is that we are doing which causes the bad effect and choose not to do it. Only choice, a restored voluntariness, will bring the change in our postural behaviour which will effect the desired improvement. While the activity remains involuntary we will go on doing it as we have always done it.

So, for voice, we have to cultivate an awareness of how we are using ourselves and of how our physical use may be interfering with the processes of good voice production. In doing this we have to look to the root causes. Probably this will mean considering more than how the organs of articulation or the throat or even the breathing mechanism are functioning. We look to the body as a functioning whole, and particularly to the way we employ our postural mechanisms. Above all we shall be concerned with the relationship which exists between the head, the neck and the back, because this will determine what we are doing with the rest of the body, including the voice.

Common misuses which affect the voice

PULLING THE HEAD BACK instead of dropping the jaw when taking a breath to speak. This has the effect of closing part of the throat and putting the larynx in a poor state of relationship with the breath. The observable movement may be small, but its inevitable consequences for voice are profound. It can lead to a lack of control of the soft palate and the production of an overly nasal tone; it can also lead to considerable strain when using the higher notes; the release of the jaw is impeded with a consequent closing of the back of the mouth and a thinness of resonance; it can provoke gasping in-breaths, and a stiffening of the tongue-root which can interfere with flexible resonation and sometimes cause problems in articulation.

PULLING DOWN is often associated with pulling the head back. It's

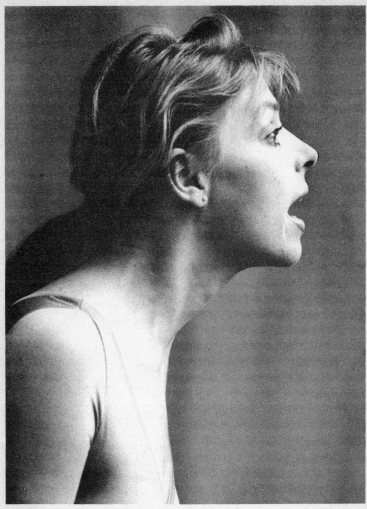

1   **How to get a sore throat**

In trying to reach the other person in the conversation the speaker has
stuck her face forward and pulled the skull off the bottom jaw –
thereby squashing the neck and throat and disconnecting the voice
energy from the supporting breath: the more energetic the impulse,
and the louder the sound, the more she will strain her voice. This
misuse is often associated with gasping.

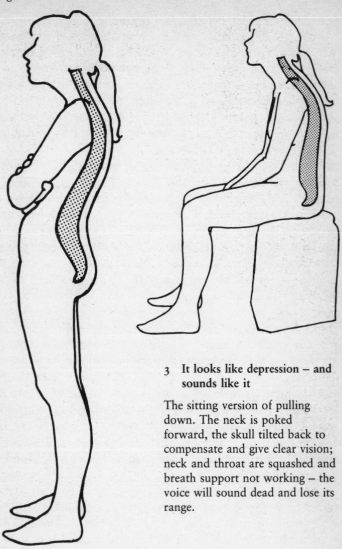

3 It looks like depression – and sounds like it

The sitting version of pulling down. The neck is poked forward, the skull tilted back to compensate and give clear vision; neck and throat are squashed and breath support not working – the voice will sound dead and lose its range.

2 Gravity wins – collapse

Everything is pulling down here; the movement of the rib-cage is restricted and supporting the voice is impossible.

a combination of happenings, as many of the common misuses are. The rib-cage slumps towards the stomach, the shoulders are pulled forward, and in consequence there occurs a narrowing across the top of the chest. Often people who pull down feel low in energy and to some extent depressed. The breathing is over-constricted and so the voice lacks adequate support. Often there is too much activity in the abdominal muscles and not enough in the muscles which move the ribs. A monotonous quality is often present in the voices of those who pull down.

PULLING THE BACK IN. Typically, those who pull the small of the back in are forced to breathe mostly in the upper chest; the relationship between the vertebrae is such that the back loses a lot of its width at the point where the lungs are largest. This makes speaking long phrases difficult. It also tends to provoke a situation where, when the speaker is under the slightest stress, too much adrenalin is produced, and he becomes excited to such an extent that vocal control almost disappears. Voice produced in these conditions is usually somewhat shrill and lacking in the richer resonances.

LOCKING THE KNEES. Quite often this goes with pulling the back in; it is associated with great tension of the abdominal muscles and this may lead to a very forced and throaty tone with an attendant over-tightening of the muscles of the glottis. The knees will be *seen* to be locked when the person is standing, but the tension which produces locked knees, coming as it does from a bad distribution of weight, will be present when the person is moving.

Some things are common to all the foregoing examples of misuse. It is noticeable that the proper head/neck/back relationship no longer exists – it has been interfered with. Also, some parts of the body are not doing their fair share of work and so other parts are forced to work too hard. It is also clear that the misuse may start in a particular part of the body, but it never remains localized there: it soon affects the whole. In all of these examples, the voice is adversely affected in its mechanical functioning; but there is a more important consideration for the actor, and that is the fact that these forms of misuse predispose the users to certain attitudes and forms of behaviour which are difficult to change fundamentally when fundamental change is desired – say in playing a role. In other

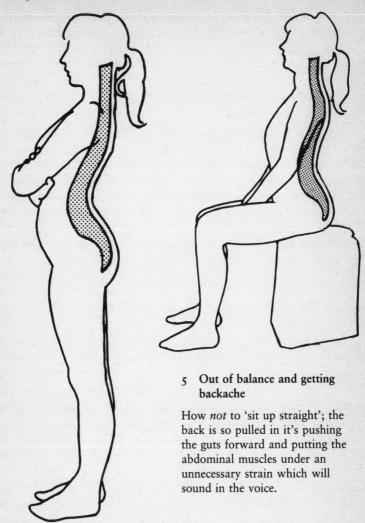

5   Out of balance and getting backache

How *not* to 'sit up straight'; the back is so pulled in it's pushing the guts forward and putting the abdominal muscles under an unnecessary strain which will sound in the voice.

4   Fighting gravity – and losing

Pulling the back in like this and locking the knees results in loss of movement in the lower ribs and provokes upper chest breathing together with an over-tense and shrill voice use.

words, actors with such misuse tend to be fixed and therefore predictable. (See pp. 186–8, The postural fix and predetermined interpretation.)

What is good use?

Good use exists when the effort needed to perform a task, whether it's lifting a bucket of concrete, sitting in a chair, or producing the voice, is just sufficient for the performance of that task. For this to happen, the body has to be in a good state of balance, where every part makes its proper contribution to the action of the whole. This comes from the relationship between the head, the neck and the back. To obtain good use we must be free from habitual responses which don't allow us to react efficiently to what's going on, so the term normally implies the use of choice as well.

Self-observation

At this point it will be useful if you spend some time observing yourself. Spend a couple of days on it before you go any further with the voice work.

When you walk past shop windows, use the opportunity to see what shape you are, how your weight is balanced, whether you lean forward or backward, or both.

Use mirrors. It is especially useful if you can arrange the mirrors so that you have a good full-length view of yourself from the sides as well as the front.

Talk; recite a poem; or tell yourself a story. What happens as you begin the action of talking?

Look at the base of your skull and the tip of your nose: do they alter their axis in space in any way?

When you open your mouth do you throw your head back? When you stand do you lock your knees or your stomach muscles?

Do you have an irregular breathing pattern, sometimes stopping the breath altogether while you think, or while waiting to speak to someone?

Try to catch yourself by surprise during conversations. When you are talking and you want to breathe do you have to gasp?

Do you as a matter of habit keep your jaw clenched or your tongue pushing up against the roof of the mouth except while you eat and talk; or perhaps even *while* you eat and talk?

When you speak, if you put a fingertip to the underside of the jaw in the V between the bone and just in front of the neck, do you feel a pressure there, as if the muscle is pushing against your finger?

If you wear glasses, does this make you want to lift the nose in order to balance them?

What happens to you as you sit down?

What, in a word, can you find out about your habits of use?

The head/neck/back relationship

Nearly all vertebrates lead their movement with the head. The body of man is designed to function this way as well. Unlike other vertebrates, however, man has the power to abandon this way of behaving; or at least seriously to interfere with it. As a creature his pre-eminent skill is adaptability, and, as we've noted, if adapting to his environment means making changes in himself which in the long term may be personally harmful, often he will make them.

It is the relationship between the head and the spine which makes for balance or imbalance. One of the functions of the inner ear is to provide information to the brain about our state of balance, and in the *normal* way of things the brain responds by giving the head the necessary direction to maintain or achieve balance; and the direction taken by the head is relayed via the spine to the rest of the body.

This vertebrate quality of leading with the head can be seen very clearly in the movement of snakes: the body usually follows exactly wherever the head has been. A cat jumping on to a table may provide another worthwhile study. When it begins its jump, the cat can't see the top of the table; before it jumps it gathers its quarters under it; then its head darts forward in the trajectory of the jump and the rest of the body follows; when it reaches the height of the table it may see that there is a clutter of objects which makes landing where it had intended too difficult; it is in such a moment that you may see the head and neck extend forward a second time, and, without any further leverage from the hindquarters, the cat manages to extend its jump to a safe place on the table; or you may see it change its mind, turn the head, and, the body following, land front feet first on the ground again.

What the cat and the snake do all the time and without seeming to have to work it out, we find more difficult. Perhaps if we wore our faces at the top of our spinal columns, like the cat, it would be a lot easier for us to lead with the head. But there is a difference between us and the cat which complicates things for us. We are bipedal. Our face points in the direction we are normally going – forward – as with the cat, but unlike the cat our spine is going up. So we have two directions operating simultaneously all the time: *forward*, the way our face points, and *up*, the way our spine points.

Unfortunately for us, if we try to simplify matters by abandoning one of these directions in the balance of the skull, imbalance results. If the action of the eyes and face take the head too far forward of the spine we lose balance and have to correct the loss either by letting the head go back where it properly belongs, or by stiffening various bits of ourselves, or by pushing a bit of us back to compensate for the bit which is too far forward. All that is fine and shows how flexible our balancing act can be; but if we *fix* in one of these compensating postures so that it becomes habitual, things begin to go fundamentally wrong and we lose our flexibility. Such a thing might easily happen to someone who is short-sighted, for example. He experiences difficulty with his eyes and it is upon the functioning of the eyes that his attention fixes; he pushes forward with his head in order to see better; he is probably not aware that in consequence he has pushed his rib-cage down and made his legs stiff to cope with the new shift of balance. In time this shift will become habitual, so that even if he gets a really good pair of eyeglasses which correct his vision and make it no longer necessary for him to peer forward, he does not make the corresponding change in the use of his body. (For an actor any such fixing could be a disaster, because it would tend so to dictate his body behaviour that his behaviour as an interpreter would be limited in turn.)

So here we have arrived at the first major point in good use: the head is facing forward but going up.

Because the head is to go up, the neck must be free enough in its articulation to allow that to happen. If we hold the neck stiffly contracted or collapsed the flexibility necessary in adjusting the direction and balance of the skull is lost. Losing this we lose any chance of good balance in the rest of the body, because it is through the neck that the direction of our balance is transmitted. A more obviously vocal point is that if the bones of the neck are in poor relationship to each other the breathing is badly affected, and so is the shape of the throat, and this will have a bad effect on resonance and tuning.

So here is the second point: the neck must be free.

The moment we release the neck so that the head, facing forward, can go up, we make it possible for the whole spine to follow the direction of the head. When this happens, the back lengthens; as it lengthens, the shoulders assume their correct placement and the rib-cage is allowed to fill its proper space. So not only does the back lengthen, but it widens.

The vertebrae are capable of tilting forward and back, and also of some degree of rotation. So the spine as a whole has great flexibility of movement. There are also natural and balanced curves in the spine, in the neck and lumbar region. What tends to happen if we lose the guiding direction of the head, however, is an exaggeration of the tilt between the vertebrae, in one direction or other, and there is a consequent exaggeration of the curves of the spine, or the loss of the curve in one direction and a compensation in another. That is why, when the correct and balanced relationship in the spine is achieved there is a lengthening.

So to encapsulate all this let us say:

The neck must be free
So that the head can face forward and go up
So that the back can lengthen and widen.

Legs and feet

As the back lengthens and widens, following the direction of the head, you will notice a new relationship developing with the legs and feet. In order to keep the back working well it is necessary not to overtighten the legs. There should be no holding of the stomach muscles, no bracing back of the knees and no clenching of the buttocks. The legs, too, take part in the new sense of direction; they are released at hip, knee and ankle, so that when you walk the transference of weight may be kept easy and smooth. If you impair the articulation of any of these joints by holding them too tight and closed, the back will suffer for it. When you stand, the joints should be as free as if you were in a state of movement. Then your weight is evenly distributed on the heels, the outer side of the feet, the balls of the feet and the toes – all of the foot in fact which goes to make the classic footprint shape.

You will also notice that the knees, since they are released, move slightly forward and over the big toes.

When you are standing in a well-balanced and well-directed state, you should feel that it is possible to move with equal ease in any direction. All other directions are contained, as it were, in the basic direction of Up.

What is this 'direction'?

It is two things. The first implies relationship with a point in space. So when we say the head is going Up, for example, it generally happens that that is in the direction of the ceiling or the sky, both of which are certainly Up, in the sense of being above us. But such points of absolute reference will not apply if we are on our hands and knees, say. Then what is Up? It is the direction the head must take to lead the spine into length. It is this Up – not where the ceiling is – which concerns us.

But in order for us to *have* direction, we must *give* direction to ourselves – we must order ourselves in the direction we wish to maintain. Unless we keep reminding ourselves what we are doing, the unconscious habits of use will reassert themselves. During this process of re-educating the body we become aware that there are

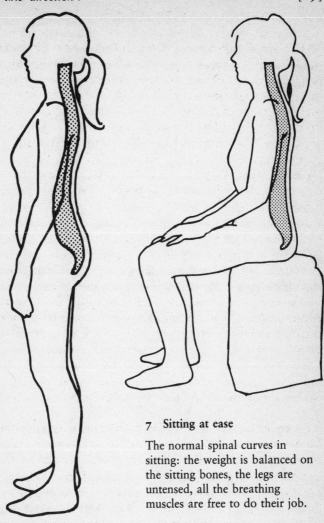

7 Sitting at ease

The normal spinal curves in
sitting: the weight is balanced on
the sitting bones, the legs are
untensed, all the breathing
muscles are free to do their job.

6 Using gravity for balance

Here the spinal curves are normal;
the lengthening of the spine
allows full flexibility in breathing,
movement and voice; in this state
of good balance every muscle and
joint is free to do what it has to
– and no more.

bits of us where the energy is wrongly distributed, muscles over-tightened where they need to be released, other muscles lacking in tonus because they are not doing their proper work, joints over-closed where they need to be allowed more freedom. This state of things is gradually corrected and what corrects it is conscious control, *direction* of energy.

Joints and muscles: not doing

If you connect a muscle to a bio-feedback device and you tell that muscle to relax, you will see the machine register an increase of tension. This happens because as soon as you draw attention to a muscle it tightens; this is the only possible response which muscle has to stimulus because muscle has no active releaser, only an active doer. The person connected to the bio-feedback machine in trying to relax the muscle is trying to *do* something with it and that is why the muscle tenses. However, after watching the needle on the dial a couple of times, he realizes that he can't relax the muscle directly and he makes, as it were, a translation of the thought 'muscle, relax' and does something else which produces the relax effect. What he does is stop tightening the muscle. In other words, a *non*-doing. The fact that sometimes in order to achieve the desired effect in an action we have '*not* to do', rather than '*do*' is not something which we know automatically. Often we have to learn it and think about it.

And what we have to think about is not so much relaxing muscles as releasing joints; because in the capsule of a joint and the surrounding ligaments are all the little receptors which feed back information to the brain and provide us with a picture of the shape of ourselves and what we are doing. We know whether we are tight or released in a joint, but we don't know in the same direct way whether a muscle is tense or not – to tell us that we need a feedback mechanism: a machine or a sensitive observer or teacher.

Often, despite the fact that we can't know directly whether or not the muscle is tense, we make *assumptions* based on the information which comes to us from the joints. These assumptions may, or may not, be correct; more often than not they are incorrect. Most of us have very faulty sensory appreciation: our kinaesthetic awareness, because of established patterns of misuse, has been led astray.

However, if you don't have a bio-feedback machine, don't despair, because it is possible to be your own observer and teacher.

Stopping

We now come to the means whereby we can exert the control which we need.

Habitual response is immediate. That is, as soon as I motivate myself to do an accustomed action, I immediately start to do it the way I am *used* to doing it. It is this immediacy of response which is the most difficult thing we have to face if we wish to make fundamental changes in our use.

We have to learn to say NO to the response and stop it from happening. Since the response comes attached to the act which provoked it, we have, in the first place to say no to the act itself. This is the major interruption of the habit. However, this does not mean giving up action! What we are doing is saying no to one set of actions while allowing another to take its place. This second set of happenings will not be habitual; in fact, until they happen you won't entirely know what they will be. That is because you will be allowing this second set of happenings to occur while keeping your directions, and at first this will feel unusual and odd.

What is happening is this: you use the process of stopping in order to refuse your muscles their accustomed reaction to stimulus; and you use direction, and permission, on the joints. That is how the new relationships are made.

A typical sequence of happenings using stopping and direction would go as follows:

1 I want to speak

2 However, every time I do so I pull my head back, and I don't wish to do that as I know it impedes the process of vocalization.

3 But this response of pulling the head back is automatic and immediate.

4 To avoid the reaction which goes with it I must cancel the message
   to speak. I think 'I will not speak' and I say to the muscles of the
   neck 'stop doing' (or 'neck be free'); this produces the effect of
   release, the bones of the neck are allowed to assume their proper
   relationship – open rather than closed. The neck, in other words,
   has been prevented from making its 'normal' speech reaction.

5 I re-affirm my direction of the whole head/neck/back relationship.

6 I keep this release with direction, and I open my jaw without
   pulling my head back.

This is a slow process at first. Re-education is. After a few moments
of talk you will probably notice that the head is being thrown back
again. Patience. Repeat the process. In time you will associate
speaking with keeping the neck free and the head well directed.
Also, the difference in the tone of the voice will alert you very soon
if you start to use yourself badly. When this occurs, don't try directly
to get the good tone back, because if you do it is likely that you will
start to *force* one use against the action of another: underneath, the
old habit will reassert itself. No, in order to put things right, go
through the whole process. It isn't a short-term change of use which
you are trying to achieve. What you are after is a basic freedom in
the whole use of your voice (and yourself). To get it and keep it, the
means whereby must be kept in use; short cuts will inevitably bring
you back to your point of departure.

Won't all this self-consciousness get in the way?

No. Not only will it not get in the way, it will render your actions
freer to fulfil your intentions, and with more speed and precision.

We may tend to think that self-consciousness is a state of acute
awkwardness produced by being suddenly in the limelight and
expected to do something alien to us. I remember an exercise in
audience contact we had to perform as drama students; we had
simply to walk on to the stage and sit down facing an audience of
fellow students. Nearly all of us found it unnerving despite the fact
we were used to being on stage in plays; we looked, and felt, about
as stiff and awkward as it is possible to be. This was the effect of

an unaccustomed and heightened self-consciousness which we didn't know how to turn to our advantage. We were so unusually aware of ourselves that we took fright. Since one of the results of fright and panic is a tendency to tighten the neck, I expect that's what we did, and consequently lost our sense of balance and co-ordination. Since you will be constantly practising a heightened form of self-awareness, and since you will be using it to achieve freedom, the more of it you have the better; and the more of it you have, the less likely you are to find yourself thrown off-course by unusual circumstances. Anyway, if we didn't have self-awareness to some degree, how on earth would we survive without getting run over or starving to death? Because it is our self-awareness in relation to our environment which warns us of the need not to step in front of the approaching car, and our self-awareness in relation to our own functioning which tells us when we need to eat. The actor or the public speaker needs to be aware of himself and his functioning; he needs to be aware of what effect he is having on his audience, and, for maximum effectiveness, he needs not only to be completely responsive to the moment in which he is, but also to have a clear awareness of the moments he has just lived so that he can judge what he needs to do to communicate more effectively in the moments about to happen. Also, in the case of the actor, an awareness of what is happening on the stage with the other actors is needed as well! This is self-consciousness of a very high order – but totally necessary if we are to make the most of the communicative moment.

What's going to happen to my spontaneity?

If by spontaneity you mean the ability to react with adaptability to the changing needs of the second – an interruption by a heckler, or an actor forgetting his lines or suddenly jumping a couple of vital pages of text, or sensing that the attention of the audience is wandering – then you will only have spontaneity more abundantly.

If, on the other hand, by spontaneity you mean that state where our unconscious motivations take control and we are being run by our habitual responses – who needs it?

We are concerned with using ourselves with judgement, which is an integral part of behaving intelligently and artistically. Using ourselves with judgement doesn't mean that we give up having the usual human responses and feelings, but that we are *choosing* how to use those responses and feelings to further our communication of whatever it is that we wish to communicate. If we refuse choice, or if as artists we are in such a state that effectively we have no choice, then we are dodging the responsibility of our humanity and artistry; which is, to say the least, a state of romantic obfuscation, and at the worst a wilful perversion.

Exercises

Floor work

One of our chief enemies in the business of achieving good use is gravity. So we have to convert it into an ally. You can do this by starting work lying on the floor on your back. Put a couple of books under your head as a support to begin with. It helps you not to tilt the head back. Don't put too many under your head or you may find you have tilted the head forward. The height of the books will depend on what you find comfortable as you proceed. If you have rather bunched-together shoulders and are inclined to poke your head forward, you may find that you need about eight or nine centimetres of book to begin with; but later, as your back opens and your shoulders move apart and flatten out, you will want to decrease that height by three or four centimetres.

You will probably find, if your legs are stretched out, that there is a gap under the small of your back. Don't try to force the back down, it will go down of its own accord as you learn to release whatever is holding it up. To help this happen, draw one leg at a time toward the body so that your knees point to the ceiling and your feet are flat on the floor. It helps if you work on a non-slip surface, otherwise you might find that you have tightened your stomach muscles to ensure that your feet don't slip; if you do this you will find yourself hanging on to your legs instead of keeping them free but directed. Your feet should be apart and so should the knees.

Your arms should be by your sides, the elbows slightly crooked to help the shoulders open. The palms of the hands may be flat on the floor, but if you are not released enough to do this easily, let the

8 Making friends with gravity

Work position: books support the head in a comfortable relationship with the neck and back; with the knees up the back can rest on the floor and the abdominal muscles are encouraged not to over-tense

palms rest on the stomach near the groin; alternatively, you could put a couple of small cushions under the wrists, or under the elbows.

While you are on the floor in this position, don't try to force anything to happen; it is better to allow things to happen as a result of your stopping and directing.

Tell yourself to keep the neck free.

Direct the head Up (in the sense that it is leading the spine to lengthen) and make sure that you are maintaining the forward direction of the head as well, which means, since you are on the floor, that your face will be in the same plane as the floor.

Allow your back to lengthen, following the lead of the head, and allow the consequent tendency to widen in the back.

Keep checking the joints and directing them to release into an open state – again, don't try to DO this release by working the muscles around the joints; you should have a sense that you are *allowing* things to happen rather than *making* them happen.

Properly performed, this process leaves you feeling wide awake, tuned up, and with plenty of energy at your command. If you find after a few minutes that you are becoming drowsy and flaccid, it is probable that you are losing your sense of direction and drifting into a state of collapse or over-relaxation.

It is a good idea to give yourself between twenty and thirty minutes a day of this work, and preferably before you do any other exercises; you will do them much better as a result. After you have been practising this routine for some time you will find a change for the better in your awareness of your head/neck/back relationship; and not only in your awareness of it, but also in its functioning.

Having spent so much time getting that relationship working, it would be a pity to throw it away by getting up badly. You might find rolling over and getting up from your hands and knees is a help. It's up to you. But keep those directions going and make sure you are leading with your head.

When you are finally standing, remember your legs. Often it is the tension in the legs which makes us throw our backs in. Again, use stopping – or inhibition – as your means whereby to stop this happening. You should, for some time, have a physical memory of the floor and your work there. Let it help you. Keep your directions going as you walk, jog, or just sit.

There are other exercises you can do on the floor before getting up, but we shall come to those later on. The work which immediately follows could be done on the floor, too, but at the beginning is best performed sitting or standing.

Whispered 'ah'

This exercise is quite difficult but is a good preparation for bringing several of the major functions together. It helps release the jaw and so ensures that a good opening of the mouth and pharynx are achieved, both necessary for adequate resonance; and in releasing the jaw the tongue is helped to release as well, so this prepares us for the work of articulation; finally it brings the breath into use in such a way that both inspiration and expiration are properly performed, using the musculature in the right way so that eventually when you come to do the breathing exercises you will find that you already have a good sense of what you are about. There are five stages of preparation before doing the exercise:

1 Check your directions and make sure the neck is free. This applies to the whole exercise and should be re-affirmed at each stage.

2 Gently bring the teeth into the bite position. The tongue should be resting lightly against the bottom front teeth, and not held narrow but allowed to spread.

3 Release the joint of the jaws and allow the lower jaw to slide forward until your top teeth rest on your lower teeth. Don't push. The tongue moves, flat and untensed, with the bottom jaw, and still rests without pushing against the lower teeth.

4 Smile. A real smile. This action of the facial muscles helps the jaw not to pull back.

5 Open the jaw, with the tongue still touching the bottom teeth as in 3, and keep the smile. The jaw is opened to the full extent you can manage without forcing.

During this sequence, make sure you don't stop breathing.

Now you have prepared the opening of the jaw and you go on to complete the exercise as follows:

1 Breathe out, whispering (which means *completely* without voice) the vowel 'Ah'. Don't try to make the breath last as long as possible, merely until it is no longer completely comfortable to breathe out. There must be no sense of pulling down at the throat and chest during expiration. *Keep your length and width going.* The opening of the mouth and the use of the tongue are the same as in the preparation, of course.

2 Close the mouth (as in stage three of the preparation) allowing the breath in through the nose. Again, don't let the release of the abdominal muscles and the ribs pull you down.

3 Check directions and the release of the neck and repeat.

With this method of working the opening of the articulation of the jaw (and the exercise should be performed a few times on each occasion you do your voice work), eventually you will find that you quite naturally and easily keep the jaw in the correct relationship with the head and neck during the act of speaking. You will not

need to use props to keep the teeth apart and to help you to find
that opening which you need. Of course, when you are speaking
you will not necessarily be smiling, or opening the teeth a great
deal; but the hinge of the jaw will be well open and that is
what counts when it comes to finding good resonance and clear
articulation of speech.

Memory patterns

The work you have done in order to achieve a good head/neck/back
relationship is clearly not something which finishes with the formal
exercise time. You are trying to achieve a permanent liberation of
your use, so you need to keep practising in ordinary life as well,
until the good use is a well-established everyday fact and quite the
normal thing for you. In order to help this along, it is a good idea
to examine your daily routine to see if there is a pattern to it and
then to make use of that pattern as part of the work.

The day, for most people, begins in the bathroom, and there you
will have a mirror. You can use it as a check while you are washing
or brushing your teeth and see if you are closing the articulations
of the hand and arm or if you begin to squash the neck.

When you bend over the basin, are you keeping the head/neck/back
relationship going? Are you using the articulations of hip, knee
and ankle to help you keep the back lengthening? Or are you
collapsing from the waist?

What happens when you have breakfast? Do you find that you are
in such a hurry that you tighten your neck to lift the cup?

If you go out to work and follow a regular route, this is an excellent
opportunity to monitor your walking. Are you rolling from side
to side as you walk? If so, you need to release a bit more in the
hip and to keep your direction of Up going. And in releasing the
hip, don't forget the head and neck. Are you holding your ankles
stiffly? Well, let them go, release them, and let the weight roll
easily through the foot from heel to toe.

With all this awareness of what you are doing to and with yourself,
don't lose awareness of what is going on around you.

Gradually you will find that an association between the work and your daily routine will establish itself, and the mere fact that you are brushing your teeth or walking to work will provoke your memory and your awareness.

One word of warning about mirrors and shop windows. They provide fairly objective evidence as to what you are doing. But there is always the temptation, if you find your mirror-image is sloping forward or slumping or has its head resolutely pulled back, to snap into action and DO a correction to the image by DOING something to yourself like pulling yourself upright or pushing the head more forward. DON'T. Work in the normal way: stop, release with direction, and allow the joints to adjust following that direction. This may be slow and unglamorous, but it is sure.

How do I know I'm right if when I feel right I'm wrong?

It all depends of course on what we mean by 'feeling right'. But for most of us it would mean feeling as we normally feel; feeling comfortable. But if we are trying to change our normal use we are quite likely to feel 'wrong' during the process of change. And further to complicate matters, as our use changes, so does our sensation and our perception of 'right' change. It is therefore difficult to know when we *are* right. But that doesn't really matter. Our sensory appreciation is always a fallible mechanism, although less fallible as the work progresses.

One positively helpful thing is that it is often much easier to know when we are wrong than when we are right. The habits of misuse we have acquired over the years become familiar and recognizable as the work increases our general self-awareness. The wrong doesn't change so confusingly as the 'right'. If I'm confirmed in the habit of pulling the head back, even when I've recognized the fact, it is likely that I'll want to go on pulling the head back – although to a lesser and lesser degree. I'm unlikely to develop a sudden addiction to twitching my kneecaps in place of pulling the head back.

This means that in practice you don't have to worry too much about how you feel; just continue with the basic work. Stop and direct. Stop and direct, until a state of re-educated functional efficiency is achieved.

But of course there is one guide you cannot ignore. As your use improves, so will your voice. If you're producing a poor or painful sound, the chances are it is largely due to bad use.

A humpback, a limp and a withered arm

So what do you do if you play Richard III? An actor will be expected to change his physical behaviour from role to role and he may do so with safety if, by nature or good training, he is predisposed to a mechanical use which is efficient. He may adopt the limp and hunchback of Richard III, but he will not necessarily therefore tighten his jaw and neck; he may find he cannot breathe with one side of his body, but he will compensate by using the other side to the full. But if to begin with his mechanical use is poor and he is unaware of a technique for making good use of his body, then the adverse conditions of use imposed by the role of Richard III will be exacerbated, and he may find that he's not just playing a cripple but is fast on the way to becoming one as tension provokes tension until in the end he loses his voice or finds he needs a course of osteopathy to straighten him out again.

A good shape in the body is the product of good use; but good use can help us make sense of even bad shapes that we may temporarily have to adopt.

Stage fright

The common advice given to someone suffering from an attack of stage fright is to take a few deep breaths, and as long as the breathing is well done this is good advice. But I'm considering stage fright here rather than in the section on breathing because at bottom it is a phenomenon produced by a disturbance of our use.

The symptoms of stage fright can be most unpleasant. There is a disturbance of the breathing cycle (see the Appendix on the anatomy of breathing); there is a disturbance of the digestive processes which in extreme cases can lead to nausea; at the same time we experience a dry feeling in the mouth and begin to sweat heavily; it is noticeable that various muscles get into a state of great tension, particularly those of the abdomen and upper chest. Also, because this is a form of panic, there tends to occur part or all of what has been described as the 'panic reflex'; this takes the form of pulling the back of the neck closed, almost as though we feared a blow to the nape of the neck. This is not surprising; stage fright occurs, as fright generally does, when we feel threatened, and our body is getting ready to fight or fly the source of the threat. But if you are just about to give a performance, you can't do either. So your body is in a state of frustration, and the chemical processes which are going on, instead of helping you adjust to a dangerous situation, just disorganize you and make the waiting time a torture. The sense of torture often goes once we are *in* the danger area, that is, on the stage, as we find a release for the abundance of energy which the fright of anticipation has produced in us, and then we may experience a reaction the other way in proportion to the severity of our reaction to danger – we may find ourselves extremely strong, quick-witted and confident in our capacity to deal with any emergency. This brings such a feeling of exhilaration to us that often it seems, despite the agonies beforehand, that life can have nothing better to offer. So stage fright can have its uses in keying-up our survival mechanisms to a fine fighting pitch.

On the other hand, people can find themselves so overwrought by the anticipation of the dangers ahead that the act of actually getting on to the stage becomes an impossibility. What are they to do in such circumstances? Let's go back and consider that panic reflex. One of the two major nerves responsible for our breathing takes as its point of origin the third, fourth and fifth cervical vertebrae. If we badly upset the relationship between these vertebrae, the uninterrupted and continuing exchange of in-breath for out-breath, the rhythmicity of our breathing cycle, is adversely affected. The other major nerve which activates our breathing starts working in overdrive, as it were, and we feel short of breath – no matter how much breath we actually have! This second nerve also supplies our digestive process, the muscles of the larynx, and the heart; hence the feeling of nausea, the rapid heartbeat and the need to keep swallowing and 'dry mouth'. So, yes, we have to re-establish the rhythmicity of our breathing, and taking a few deep, but not too deep, breaths may help; but what will help most in coping with all the nasty symptoms and keeping them under control is to free the neck and make sure the basic head/neck/back relationship is working. We won't have abolished the fright, but we will have it under control.

The Alexander Technique

Most of the work described in this chapter is based on the discoveries of F. Matthias Alexander (see Appendix 2) and the technique he evolved because of those discoveries. If it is possible for you to work with a teacher of his technique it would be a good thing to do so. But there remains, all the same, a great deal one can do by oneself to acquire good use and to prepare the body for the voice work which follows. And, after all, Alexander himself worked alone in perfecting his method of work and curing himself of his own misuses!

Further body work

This chapter hasn't exhausted the business of body work in relation to voice production; it's merely a brief introduction to the fundamentals and there's more about body use later on. The exercises described here should form part of a daily routine and it would be as well to give yourself some considerable time in working your body daily in this way before you go on to the voice work itself. However, if you don't have the time, you can go on to the voice work with good effect, but you must keep working on your use all the time, and the better your use becomes, the more you will get out of the rest of the work.

BREATHING

The normal and the athletic

Breathing for voice is not a mysterious or strange process, any more than breathing to walk down the street is, and if you have ensured that your basic use is working for you rather than against you, then in the course of using the voice normally you will experience no difficulty with the breath – providing your speech sounds are efficiently tuned (see Tuning).

The demands of the spoken theatre are such that very rarely are you called upon to produce the voice athletically, and then probably only for short bursts. Most of the actor's work in the theatre demands a voice use which sounds quite natural while at the same time it fills the performance space adequately. In most plays and in most theatres this is no great feat and largely depends upon having a basic good use.

However, even if your general use is good, you are likely to find some difficulty in sustaining an adequate use of your voice if you find yourself, say, playing in a musical, where you not only have to speak with a normal sound, but also have to dance and sing. Also, you might easily find yourself playing in a space where the acoustics make life difficult, say in the open air. So you must prepare yourself for some degree of athleticism in your voice use even if you are only going to put it to the test very rarely.

For all this, you not only need to release the breathing mechanism into correct functioning, but also to develop that mechanism so that it is strong.

The need for breath

There are three basic tasks we set ourselves as speakers and actors as far as the breath supply is concerned. The first is to ensure an adequate supply of oxygen to the blood while we go about our strenuous business. This we might call Breathing for Work. The second task is to supply enough breath at the right pressure to pass through the glottis (the gap between the vocal cords) and then between the speech organs so that we can give out enough sound to fill a theatre comfortably with clear speech; an extension of this is making sure that we have enough control to be able to use the voice athletically, say in screaming or singing, as we have noted above. To do this we need the breath to act as a good Support to the voice. The third task is to make sure that the breath is responsive to the shape of the thought we are trying to express and to the emotion that goes with the thought, and this calls for us to master the uses offered by the changeability of the breathing pattern. We shall consider these aspects of breathing one at a time.

For those who wish to clarify their thoughts on how the breathing mechanism works I have supplied a brief description of the anatomy of breathing in the Appendix on p. 223.

Oxygenation: breathing for work

The amount of oxygen that the blood requires increases in direct proportion to the work being done. It's as well to remember this so that you can train yourself to be able to perform vigorous work (such as running, jumping, dancing) and not leave yourself short of breath for the use of the voice. After all, you may have to sing and dance at the same time. If the body is not in a trained state you will find this virtually impossible without a breakdown in the rhythmicity of your breathing (see pp. 43–4). Also, if you engage in such heavy work and your body isn't used to it, the breathing muscles may get so tired because of the unaccustomed rapid deep breathing that you may find yourself beginning to get into a state of physical collapse, losing your head/neck/back relationship and generally finding you haven't enough energy to go on. There is not, so far as I know, a short cut in training to be able to do this kind of work with the control of the voice left unimpaired. Exercises are suggested later on in this chapter, but the fundamental thing is to accustom the body to moving and vocalizing at the same time.

What is 'support'?

First let us consider what it isn't, and that is any process whereby we fix part of ourself. Our support has to be able to change to cope with our changing vocal demands; any fixed system of support tends to make for an inflexible use of the voice, and inevitably it produces a rigidity in the use of the body which is no good for acting; so clenched buttocks, permanently elevated and distended rib-cages, braced knees or a forced posture of the shoulders are absolutely out.

Support for the voice is strength with direction and it comes about when the breathing muscles are working in a state of co-ordination with a good head/neck/back relationship. To put it simply, it is the refusal to collapse, and the physical means whereby you make your breath last as long as you want, at the pressure you need to make whatever sound you want, at whatever volume, pitch and resonance is called for.

As you breathe out during vocalization, the abdominal muscles shorten and pull the ribs down. If the breath is not to be pushed out in a great whoosh, the rib muscles and the muscles which support the spine need to resist this downward pull, otherwise the whole rib-cage slumps towards the stomach, the spine bows and the out-breath is uncontrolled – collapse has occurred. The important thing to note here is what is happening to the spine, because if the spine is maintaining its lengthening tendency the rib-cage cannot collapse downwards. However, the ribs are left free to move. During the out-breath, the ribs which are anchored to the spine at the back and the breast bone in the front slightly rotate (or depress) while the lower ribs move in towards the centre of the body. This has the effect of making the chest noticeably narrower from side to side and slightly narrower from front to back. But the chest is not seen to slump in the slightest, the shoulders are completely uninvolved and stay open and still. How much the ribs move will now depend

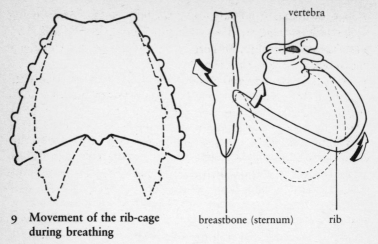

vertebra

breastbone (sternum)   rib

9   **Movement of the rib-cage
during breathing**

Solid lines show the rib-cage
expanded at in-breath; broken
line shows rib-cage after out-
breath

10   **Direction of rib movement
during breathing**

on the intrinsic strength of the rib muscles and the quality of sound
you wish to make from moment to moment.

How the quality of the desired sound affects the breathing is all
thoroughly considered in the section on Tuning, but it is as well to
note here in passing that the action of the diaphragm during
vocalization is also extremely variable and changes according to
the quality of voice. In the normal conversational use of the voice
the diaphragm usually behaves in much the same way that it does
for an unvocalized out-breath, that is to say it maintains its upward
movement in a condition of passivity; the louder and firmer the
vocalization, the more the diaphragm asserts its own specific
tendency which is to flatten as for the in-breath. This action helps
to keep the air pressure at the glottis exactly right for the loudness
of the sound – neither too much (which would provoke a breathiness
of tone) nor too little (which would produce a withheld quality to
the voice).

During vocalization, then, there is a constant interplay between
the abdominal muscles, the muscles of the rib-cage and the whole
of the back and the muscles of the larynx. All of these organs will

change their state from moment to moment; what will not change is the basic co-ordination which comes from the continuing head/neck/back relationship. This provides the direction, and training of the muscles provides the strength.

The whole question and practice of support is a vexed one in the world of voice production. Some of the more bizarre methods, those which use states of fixity for example, have usually evolved as means of forcing an unprepared body to make the desired quality of sound. They are systems of compensation for mechanisms which are basically not working well. No good use of the voice can have as its basis a system of compensation such as this. Good voice use must come from the co-ordinated good use of the body as a whole.

Changeability

Possibly one of the reasons for the proliferation of breathing techniques in voice work is the fact that there are so many possible ways of performing the act. The equipment is so designed that variability of its use is part of our natural adaptability to changing circumstances. We change our breathing in response to emotion, and each emotion has its breathing pattern – a fact used by psychiatrists and doctors in the diagnosis and treatment of several kinds of disturbance. Lying can be detected through changes in the breathing pattern. Different physical activities call for differences in the breathing. The changing chemical state of the body, the presence of viruses and some bacteria, sensations such as heat or cold – all these will affect the way we breathe. And, most importantly from our point of view, our breathing changes in response to our desire to express a thought or an emotion in words and sounds. In other words, the accuracy of our motivation for a line or phrase will affect our ability to give it breath in the right way.

If the body changes its breathing to accommodate each change of self in relation to stimulus whether from without or within, why bother to train the breathing system? Why not just leave it to get on with the job? Because most of those changes do not necessarily produce the conditions in the vocal equipment which enable us to communicate adequately the change of state in question. Or rather, the use of voice which in ordinary life might communicate the changing state of the speaker probably wouldn't fill a theatre and communicate the same information to the audience. Our ability to communicate whatever it is we wish to communicate is of paramount importance and that is not the same, particularly in the theatre, as merely *experiencing* the thing to be communicated. The experience is only the start, and in some cases of course we cannot reasonably be expected to have experienced in detail what we communicate. I should imagine that very few have experienced the act of killing a king, but that doesn't mean that Macbeth is unplayable.

It is all a matter of processing the information and choosing how we use it. It is the same problem as playing Richard III. Or, for example, playing a character in an advanced state of terror. Normally this would mean the breathing would be in a state of great agitation with the upper chest working more than the lower part of the rib-cage. Can we do it? Yes, of course; but if we want the voice to carry and fill the theatre we have to make sure that we don't block the throat or produce so much saliva that we are in danger of drowning or so little that we can only croak. We keep our consciousness functioning and with it our control. We do not allow our breathing to get into a fix or a state of breakdown, and to do this we make sure to keep the neck free. In the heat of the acting moment? Yes, in the heat of the acting moment. Because we are using the upper chest to do most of the breathing we will very likely find that we run out of effective breath after fairly short phrases. On a naturalistic level and with such a text, this would be a help; but what if the speech expressing the fear is not naturalistically phrased and doesn't allow for short breaths? Again it's a question of selection; we can't take short breaths, we have to use the whole rib-cage freely, but we know that when we're in a state of terror the voice tends to rise in pitch and we can make it do that; we know there tends to be an uncertainty in the quality of resonance which implies that our breathing is not under control, and we can do that, even though our breathing is perfectly under control. This is where artifice helps, and is necessary. The whole business of the theatre lies in its ability to communicate truth about the human condition through artifice. Actually putting the thing itself on stage – in this case a terrified person – doesn't ensure communication, about terror or anything else.

It may seem from this that I am advocating a cold, calculating and passionless state of being as the acting state. Nothing could be further from the truth. The mere act of acting is highly charged with emotion and needs to be if it is to create a state of involvement between the actor and the audience. That is all the more reason for the actor to become expert in managing himself and his emotions so that he can exercise his craft with judgement. What distinguishes the actor's passion in the heat of the acting moment from the passions he experiences in ordinary life is that it is always coupled with his desire and need to communicate it to the audience. This implies a high degree of consciousness. The greater his consciousness, the greater his ability to choose how he will use his passion and his whole means of expression – himself.

Common breathing problems

Not being able to get the voice out

This is a form of shortness of breath which happens because the speaker, probably nervous in case he runs out of breath, takes a huge in-breath and locks it in the chest; thereafter he is reduced to breathing with a restricted movement of the diaphragm and feels, naturally enough, short of breath; he probably also feels constricted in the throat and produces a strangled sort of tone, and an overly glottic attack in the voice. Again this is part of the locking process; the breath is at great pressure and the larynx closes so that the air won't escape; but on the other hand, some breath has to get through the larynx or there won't be any sound at all. So war is set up, a state of spasticity is arrived at and generally the actor suffering from this condition goes beetroot red and looks and sounds in imminent danger of a heart attack. This problem is easily solved by working on the release mechanism of the breathing, as in the later exercises.

Running out of breath

This is the commonest trouble encountered by actors and speakers and can happen for the following reasons:

1 Damage to the breathing system caused by illness, smoking etc.
2 The phonation or tuning (see pp. 59–111) is poor and so too much air escapes on all the speech sounds.

3 This is a more selective business than the foregoing example but is basically the same thing: too much pressure is put upon the consonants, particularly the unvoiced consonants, and in consequence too much breath is used to break the muscular barrier imposed by the speech organs. We shall consider this problem in the section on Speech.

4 The use of the body is such that the lungs cannot achieve a full expansion, because the rib-cage is slumped, or the back is closed, or because the muscles responsible for elevating and depressing the ribs are underdeveloped. This has been considered in the previous section on Body Use, but there are some exercises in this section as well.

5 A very common reason for running out of breath is that the muscles which control the out-breath are held in a partial fix at the end of expiration and so the proper expansion of the chest is not achieved during the in-breath. This leads to another common problem: the audible gasp, which is pretty bad in the theatre but a nightmare during any microphone work.

Not being able to get the voice out and the last mentioned way of running out of breath have in common that they are states of fixity; the Fix deserves a section to itself.

The fix and the gasp

In using the breath normally, and well, the intake is silent, and when we are speaking or otherwise using the voice, it is quick. The throat during the in-breath is a clear and untense channel for the breath and this is reflected in its outward appearance which is calm and shows very few signs that a breath is being taken; there might be a movement of the larynx, and if we have been using the voice at great pressure a generally more peaceful aspect to the outer tissues of the neck than during the voiced out-breath. We should not see a great tensing in the sterno-cleido-mastoid muscle (which goes from the top of the breast bone between the collarbones to the mastoid process behind the ear); still less should we see veins and arteries extruding themselves in the neck. But this peaceful activity of the in-breath is not possible if we allow our breathing muscles to get into one of the two states of fixity mentioned above.

If we fix the out-breath muscles at the end of expiration then we have somehow to break that fix, at least partially, in order to get in the air again; and if at the same time we are not allowing the out-breath muscles fully to release, we have to force the process and this results in the gasp. The same would apply when we fix the in-breath muscles, but then the gasp is somewhat different.

The gasp is a noisy and inefficient way of taking breath, and it doesn't at all help us to keep the voice under control – by which I mean of course free to do with as we wish. It is a sign that the breathing system is breaking down; it is a last-ditch attempt to save a situation which is going horribly wrong and is leading the speaker towards a state of spasm in which he won't be able to breathe at all, because the contraction of one set of muscles is being held when it should be released in order for the other set of muscles to take over and fully draw the air in. The gasp does not put this situation right; the in-breath with the gasp is a grudging affair and nearly always provokes bad phonation as well. In extreme cases, the gasp causes the speaker to throw his head back and this can lead to a severe misplacement of the whole breathing apparatus, and if the demands made upon the gasper's voice are out of the ordinary he may find that this misplacement causes him to lose his voice.

Another effect of the fix and gasp technique, is that it interferes with the basic rhythmicity of the breathing pattern. I have mentioned rhythmicity before and it is time to clarify what I mean by the term and why it is important in the business of voice production.

Rhythmicity in breathing

This is not to be confused with breathing to a regular rhythm. It is the mode of functioning of the centres of inspiration and expiration in the brain, and we can maintain the state of rhythmicity while breathing to all sorts of rhythms (see also the section on The Nerves in Appendix 1). Rhythmicity in this case means the free and continuing exchange of impulses to breathe in or breathe out in these respiratory centres. If we break this system of regular exchange, not only do we have to gasp to get our breath in, but the gasp itself is likely to be less and less efficient as a means of ventilation; we take less and less air until a moment comes, if we are still trying to speak, when we have to take an enormous breath because we are not

sufficiently disposing of our carbon dioxide, or we are not oxygen-
ating the blood enough. This enormous breath is usually taken high
in the chest, we find we can't control the outflow and suddenly need
to sigh or bellow to use the breath, which we now have but at too
great a pressure for us to be able to cope with. However long or
short the phrase we have to speak, we have to learn how to do it
without destroying this basic rhythmicity, and to do it we have to
find a better way of taking our breath than by gasping. Such a way
is open to us by way of the release.

The release

This is exactly what it says. The hard work in breathing, surprisingly,
is not breathing in but breathing out. We have a basic predisposition
to breathe in which makes that part of the breathing cycle relatively
easy for us. Our response to danger tends to be to breathe in, even
when we have enough breath for normal purposes of ventilation.
You may see this effect in someone learning to swim; the brain has
a message that the person is in danger of drowning and its response
is to keep on breathing in; the problem in learning to breathe for
swimming, therefore, is to breathe out – much like the problem
encountered by the nervous speaker who takes a huge breath and
then won't let it go in case he never gets another one! If such a state
of fixity comes about we have to use our consciousness to stop the
muscles of breathing from going on tensing and we have to direct
ourselves in the normal way, and think into the articulations of the
ribs and direct them to release. But this is to assume the worst has
happened. A better way of going about things is never to get into
the fix in the first place and this we do by working on the breathing
as the exercise section below demonstrates.

Observing the body

One of the things which may help you in the course of the breathing
exercises which follow is to use a mirror and watch for the outward
signs which indicate that the breath control is about to go wrong.
You should particularly look for any signs that you are pulling

down while breathing out, or, for that matter, when you release to breathe in. You should also look for signs of the opposite extreme, an increase in the lumber curve, bracing of the knees, a pulling up of the clavicles, and an unpeaceful neck. At all stages during the breathing exercises, however hard you are working, the neck should stay peaceful. Various things will go on with the ribs and the abdominal muscles according to the strength of the out-breath, but don't be too alarmed; as long as you maintain your length and your sense of widening, even when you are breathing out, what happens with the ribs and the abdominal muscles will be right.

To cite a couple of the most confusing and apparently contradictory examples may help. You are likely to find when you use the breath as for talking at an ordinary volume that the ribs and the abdominal area contract at the same time: that is to say that there is an overall reduction of volume as the abdominals pull inward and the ribs are depressed. You get thinner. However, when you make a sound which is a bit louder than normal you may notice that the area of the abdomen between the arch of the ribs seems reluctant to go in straight away, and perhaps the ribs are a little slower in depressing. Take this a stage further and shout and you may see the area between the costal arch jump forward and the ribs spring outward, while the lower part of the abdomen contracts inwards. This is all a question of air control.

If the air, because it suddenly comes under great muscular pressure, as when you shout, all goes rushing out between the vocal cords, it is likely to cause them to malfunction, and at the least the mucus lining of the cords will be upset and you will find you have a sore throat. When you have to make a loud sound you must have the means to regulate the air pressure, and this is something which the larynx and the breathing muscles do between them. Hence, since the volume and pressure of the breath is changing all the time and so is the volume of the voice, you are likely to find corresponding changes in the shape of the abdominal muscles and the rib-cage. Keep your length and direct into width and don't worry unless you start feeling a strain.

One last word on self-observation before we move on to the exercises: when you use the voice the behaviour of the breathing muscles differs from when you merely breathe and do not vocalize. This is because the vocal cords are comparatively wide apart when

you do not phonate and are to some degree closed when you speak.
Remember this when you come on to do the phonation exercises.

Exercises

Introduction

This is a basic rule: don't take your breathing (in-breath or out-
breath) beyond the limit of comfort, but while you are working
always work *to* that limit.

Watch that you do not provoke a pulling down in the neck muscles;
there should never be a feeling of the throat being congested.

Once your shoulders are in a good relationship with the spine and
thorax they shouldn't need to move – but be sure you are not
fixing them to prevent such movement. The arms should be able
to move quite freely.

The slide: stage 1

This is performed on the floor, and can form a continuation of the
floor work in Body Use.

Begin with your knees up and your head on a couple of books as
for the other floor work.

Check your directions and free your neck.

Maintaining an inhibition in the abdominal muscles against tensing,
and without forcing, keeping your back flat on the floor and
directing all of the action *from* your back, allow one foot to slide
on the floor away from your body until your whole leg is down.

Still keeping the abdominal muscles from tightening, bring the leg
back to its original position again.

Do the same with the other leg.

Do the same with both legs at the same time.

Throughout, breathing should be normal – smooth and uninterrupted. The movement of the legs should be slow, smooth and

controlled, with no sudden bumps and lurches as gravity takes over from direction.

The purposes of this exercise are: to make sure you are not holding the abdominal muscles unnecessarily tensed in order to support the legs (you can feel with your fingers to see if you are in fact contracting the abdominal muscles more than is usual in ordinary breathing); also to help with the opening of the back and making room for the breath.

At no stage should anything be forced: do what you can do comfortably. As time goes on you will perform the exercise better and better. Probably at first you will have to choose between keeping the back in unforced contact with the floor and sliding the legs the whole way; in this case opt for the flat back.

The slide: stage 2

Keeping The Slide in action, release the tongue and jaw forward but keeping the teeth fairly close together (as for stage three of the Whispered 'Ah'), purse the lips in a shape halfway between [b] and [v], and, keeping the pressure of breath constant, blow out a slow stream of air until the moment comes when you want to start pulling down at the neck and collar bones.

Stop breathing out, release the abdominal muscles and the *whole* back so that the ribs are allowed to expand to their maximum without forcing.

As you repeat the exercise you will notice that this maximum increases, particularly as you allow the upper ribs play; the maximum movement of the ribs is always to the side and if you find sudden bulges in your front it is probable that you are partly bringing the back off the floor and are at the same time losing some of the lateral movement which you need for full expansion. If this happens, again, don't force your back down, direct the opening of the ribs from the spine, allow the back down to the floor. Repeat the cycle about a dozen times.

It is important not to lose length during this exercise. You will know you are losing length if you begin pulling the pelvic girdle up towards the ribs or, at the other end, if you start pulling the rib-cage down towards the pelvis. Be careful that you do not allow the release of out-breath muscles to be so violent that it disturbs your head/neck/back relationship; your head stays quietly on the books, neither pulling back nor tipping forward to constrict the throat.

Sometimes it helps to preserve length and avoid the pulling down effect if you think of the breath as being directed up from the feet during the out-breath. If this makes you hang on to your legs, then direct the outgoing air-stream from the groin upwards. If you find you have a tendency to lift the back from the floor during this exercise then a very effective way of thinking of the outgoing breath is as if it were passing through a tube from the top of the pubis through the viscera and upwards to join the spine where the lowest pair of ribs are articulated, thence the airstream is directed up the length of the spine, it passes over the hard palate (across the roof of the mouth) and thence out between the lips. (This is an image which quite often is of considerable help when it comes to developing a strong support.)

At this stage it is as well to introduce the whispered 'Ah' and perform the exercise three or four times. You will find that there is a gravitational pull on the jaw as you release it; keep the directions going and don't allow the jaw to fall back upon your throat or your tongue to slide back down your throat – keep the tongue gently touching the lower front teeth as normal in this exercise.

The monkey: introduction

This exercise is performed standing. While you were on the floor your back was straight and well open by the time you finished the exercises. Now you have to make a transition between lying down and standing, but without losing the back. Once you are erect, the curves proper to the spine when you are standing will be there, but you must not let them become exaggerated or your general use, and with it your breathing, will suffer. This exercise, which is only a prolongation of the way we use the body when we begin the act of sitting, and do it properly, is a good means of helping the transition from the floor work to the standing work. It helps you to keep and develop the openness of the back you need for adequate inspiration. It has to be practised with careful self-observation, and if you can place a couple of mirrors so that you can get a clear view of yourself from the side without having to turn your head to do so you will find it a great help. Alternatively, you might find a friend to keep an eye on you – always provided that the friend knows what to look for!

The monkey: stage 1

It is useful for this stage to have a fixed mark at the height of the top of your head to work from; a mark on the wall behind you which is reflected in the mirror or a mark on the mirror itself will serve very well. The mark provides you with objective evidence as to whether you are *actually* maintaining your height; it is quite possible to *feel* that you are without that being the case.

Standing, keeping your directions going, allow the knees to bend forward over the toes – the feet are apart.

Keep the sense of going up and do not allow yourself to lose height.

Keep letting your knees go until you reach the point at which you must lose height – but of course, don't lose your sense of direction into length!

Breathing is normal, smooth and uninterrupted.

The monkey: stage 2

Now you *are* going to lose height and you can ignore the mark; but don't lose the lengthening direction. In fact renew all the basic directions to yourself – the neck to be free so that the head can continue to lead up while facing forward, so that the spine can lengthen and the back widen.

Allow your knees to go on bending while you keep your back vertical – which it will be if it is really following the direction of the head. Continue so until you reach the point at which maintaining balance becomes difficult.

Keep your breathing normal and uninterrupted.

The monkey: stage 3

Allow your nose to drop a fraction and, maintaining the forward and up (lengthening the spine) direction of the head, bend the knees more while the body tilts *from the hip joint*.

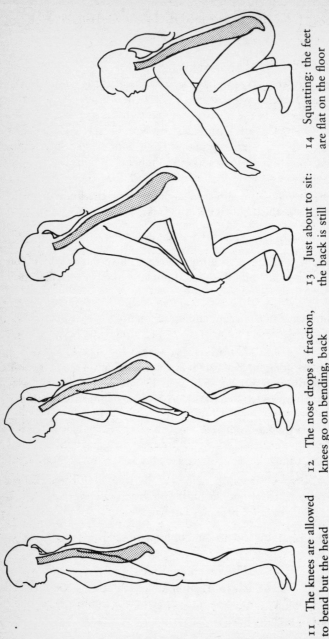

11 The knees are allowed
to bend but the head
continues to give a
lengthening direction
to the back

12 The nose drops a fraction,
knees go on bending, back
continues lengthening, torso
inclines from the hip joint

13 Just about to sit:
the back is still
lengthening

14 Squatting: the feet
are flat on the floor
and there is still no
overall loss of length

Balance breath and the back: The Monkey

Your back, although straight, is no longer vertical and is moving down in an inclined plane towards a squatting position.

Your arms hang freely.

This is a state of *balance* and there should be no pulling and pushing with the legs and feet.

Keep breathing normally.

The monkey: stage 4
Now, keeping the feet flat on the floor, continue down until you have arrived at a full squat. You may experience some discomfort in the hamstrings at first if, through poor use, they are accustomed to being in a shortened state.

Don't force; do what you can. Repetition will help the process of release and balance until you have achieved both.

The monkey: stage 5
Sitting. If you have a seat handy, try sitting from the monkey position. This means that at some time during the previous stage your bottom will have reached the level of the seat and you will come out of the squatting motion at that point. The only difference between the monkey and sitting is that once your bottom has reached the seat, you pass from one state of balance to another. Instead of your feet supporting your weight, that is now borne by your sitting bones (the ischial tuberosities). The exchange is effected as, following your head, you bring yourself to the upright position of the torso. With the exception of the angle of the feet to the legs, this is to all intents and purposes the same position as that you adopted on the floor for your first exercises. The exchange is absolutely smooth and at no stage are you out of balance, so you do not arrive on the seat with a bump, no matter how low it is. It is leading with the head which ensures your balance and so there is still no pulling and pushing with the legs or feet.

The monkey: stage 6
Now we go back to Stage 3. And be careful to follow your head and not to pull the back in.

You should find in this position that your back is wide open as it was in the floor work. Your breathing should be allowed to react accordingly and fill the whole space of your back where the lungs are.

In this position, try the whispered 'Ah' a few times. Be very careful not to pull down in the front while you do so.

The monkey: stage 7

Now, with a sense of where your back is, come up again, keeping the knees free and in no way pushed back – as in Stage 1.

Continue with full back breathing as you do so.

During the performance of The Monkey as part of your regular routine, the stages of squatting and sitting can be left out.

Whole back breathing

The sensations experienced during whole back breathing will vary from person to person to some extent. Probably, however, you will feel a widening under your shoulder blades and a widening in the lower back where the last five pairs of ribs are. You will find that these exercises encourage the lateral movement of the ribs and discourage the clavicular pull which brings the rib-cage up in front but at the cost of losing the back. If your habit has been to breathe clavicularly you may *feel* short of breath, but it is very unlikely that you actually will be. The sensation is caused by a reduced pressure in the throat, and the fact that the larynx is in an unaccustomed state of freedom while being used as a passage for the breath.

The jump-turn

While you are in the position for the Monkey at the end of Stage 2, with your knees bent but the torso still erect, following and maintaining the direction of the head, allow yourself to bounce up and down a few times.

Keep your breathing normal.

Then, still leading with the head, continue the upward bounce into a vertical jump and turn round in midair so that you land facing the opposite way. You should be so well directed and balanced at all times that when you arrive back on the floor there is no sense of having to adjust your balance.

Do this a few times, and then try making a complete turn in midair so that you land facing the way you began. Again, the same applies: you shouldn't need to adjust your balance as you land. It really is as if the motive power for these jumps is provided by the head, and not the legs and feet.

Later on you can add noise to the Monkey and the Jump-Turn, but at the moment it is enough that we are working on the balance, the co-ordination, and developing the breathing with the back.

Conducting the orchestra

This is another standing exercise. It should not be performed until you have a good working knowledge of your back. The purpose of it is to encourage the lengthening and widening while you develop the capacity for slow out-breath and quick in-breath. This is a pattern which is most necessary for speech, and is one which most people have some difficulty with, usually for the reasons we have discussed above in the section on common breathing problems.

Stand well, keeping your directions and keeping your knees released.

Imagine you are facing an orchestra which you are about to conduct.

As a conductor might, raise your arms (but keep your shoulders free) so that your hands lead out from the body, forward and wide apart as if to encompass the whole area occupied by the orchestra.

Eventually you arrive at the position in the illustration.

While you are raising your arms, look round the orchestra as if to make sure that everyone is ready, allowing your head to turn freely as you do so.

While you are raising your arms you breathe OUT.

At the apogee of your movement, and the end of your expiration, which should happen simultaneously, some idiot in the back row of your orchestra drops his instrument and destroys the whole careful preparation of the entry.

15 Conducting the orchestra

Front view showing shoulders dropped but arms fully extended at the end of expiration

16 Conducting the orchestra

Side view showing the back retains its proper curves and is not pulled
in – nor are the knees locked

Your reaction is immediate – fixing a beady eye of censure on the offending player, you DROP your arms to your sides. You are still at your full length and despite your annoyance with the idiot in the back row you still have your neck free.

As you drop your arms, you RELEASE the abdominal muscles and the ribs and allow a full breath in. This takes about the same time as it takes you to drop your arms, although, at first, it may take longer if you are not used to releasing quickly. The intake of breath is silent.

Immediately you change your motivation and begin the cycle again.

If you find it difficult to perform this exercise without pulling your back in, there is a preparation which can be done as part of the floor work.

While you are lying down with your knees up as usual, *as you breathe out*, extend the arms sideways on the floor, and, keeping them in contact with the floor, move them up until they are above your head and parallel to each other.

As you release for the in-breath, sweep the arms back to the sides.

Repeat until it is easy to do this with the back comfortably flat on the floor.

Then repeat with The Slide.

Later, during the conducting exercise you can add singing or spoken words to the outbreath, which should be as slow and controlled as you can let it be without forcing.

Clearly, Conducting the Orchestra is as much an exercise for acting as for breathing, and it should be treated as such. The more you can integrate the use of yourself as an actor with this technical preparation the better. Certainly, once we come to use the voice itself we must bring the imagination into play to motivate the sounds we are making; otherwise the noise we produce will be lifeless and detached from the communicative impulse. In turn, when we come to the business of communicating with voice and speech, if we have practised without this always in mind, we shall find our preparatory work is largely irrelevant. We shall be using ourselves in such a different mode then that we shall find it difficult to make a connection with the voice use we had in the exercises.

Blowing out candles

The last in this series of exercises will be developed in the Tuning and Speech sections. This is a preparation for the work which will follow. It is also a continuation of the quick in-breath technique.

Standing, sitting or walking, keeping your length and always with the neck free, blow out a bullet of air and *immediately* allow the breathing-out muscles to release so that the air is taken in again by the action of the breathing-in muscles.

A good way to do this is to imagine that you are blowing out candles. Put them in different places and at different distances from yourself.

When you expel the puff of air to blow the candle out, make sure you have focused exactly on where the candle is.

Don't let your head jump in that direction, however; keep your head/neck/back relationship even if you are turning the head to look in the direction of the candle. In other words – keep your neck free.

The out-breath is a vigorous short puff, and you will probably find that you want to pull down in front as you do it. To avoid this, direct the air in the manner previously described, as if it is starting from the pubis, passing up and back into the spine, continuing up the spine and so to the mouth.

Eventually you should find yourself able to direct as many puffs of air as you like and with great rapidity, taking one breath for each puff. But there are two states to be avoided. One is when you *suck* air in; this will lead to a build-up of too much air. The other, which is easier to fall into, is when you do not release properly between each out-breath. The result of this is that you contrive a rapid series of puffs of out-breath, but each time you take less air in than you have used; this will force you, every now and then, to take a supplementary 'filling breath'. In this way you come to disturb the whole breathing cycle. If you do release completely between each puff, you will find that you have taken in exactly the amount of breath that you have expelled, so an equilibrium is maintained and you can go on blowing out candles till Doomsday without strain, and without running short of breath.

A word of caution

The *way* in which these exercises are performed is more important than the mere fact of doing them. If we study to use the right means while we are working, the ends will look after themselves to a large extent. Be prepared for surprises; the voice you know as yours will change as you change the means of producing the voice. Until the means have been properly established and come into regular use, the end – the whole voice in a state of release – is a largely unknown commodity.

Maintain length, the free neck, and your basic directions. Only thus will you arrive at full width.

Force nothing.

TUNING

What is tuning?

While we are speaking or singing, the breath, passing upward from the lungs and through the trachea, or windpipe, meets an obstruction in the larynx; this obstruction is formed by the vocal cords as they come together, more or less, according to the sound. This variable opening between the cords is called the glottis. The glottis works upon the breath to produce two of the fundamental qualities of the voice: the pitch (or note) and the volume (how loud or quiet it is); this is the process of phonation. The third fundamental quality in the voice is its resonance (or timbre) and is determined partly by the action of the vocal chords and also by what happens to the phonated airstream after it passes the vocal cords and enters the resonators, chiefly those of the throat (or pharynx), the mouth and the nose. So the tuning of the voice is the outcome of how we use these three qualities of pitch, volume and resonance. This, in fact, is Voice. Later we shall see what effect the different speech sounds can have upon the voice, but at the moment it is as well to consider the voice by itself without the complications which the act of articulation may introduce; in this way we shall be better prepared to make the best vocal use of the speech sounds when we come to them.

The whisper

Not all sound in ordinary speech is produced by the action of the cords, however. Various consonants have no voice whatever and this is a part of their intrinsic quality: for example, [f] or [s]. These unvoiced consonants are formed in the same way that we whisper.

We can whisper all of the speech sounds. When we do so, the vocal cords are wide apart and offer little resistance to the breath-stream, which passes directly, unvoiced, through the resonators and past the organs of articulation. Each speech sound has its own shape, made by the organs of articulation; as speech-shape gives place to speech-shape the sound of the whisper changes. The pitch of the whisper is determined only by the size of the resonating cavities. If you whisper a phrase using your mouth as you normally do for speech, and then whisper the same phrase while holding the mouth in a yawning shape, you will hear the note of the whisper drop and this tells you that the airstream is passing through a larger cavity or resonator. In this way the sound of the whisper will prove a useful guide when you come to work for maximum resonance in the voice; it will help you know whether the resonators of mouth and throat are as large and unobstructed as they need to be to produce the fullest quality of sound.

Anatomy

In order to understand how we produce and control the tuning of the voice we shall take a brief look at the mechanism responsible for the work.

The larynx

The larynx is a moveable arrangement of cartilages, one of which, the thyroid, or Adam's apple, is so prominent that you can feel it protruding in the front of your throat. The larynx acts as a valve which, when shut, completely blocks off the lungs from the mouth. In this way it can prevent food getting into the lungs, and can control the flow of air between the lungs and the mouth and nose. This function has been adapted for voice and speech purposes in the following way.

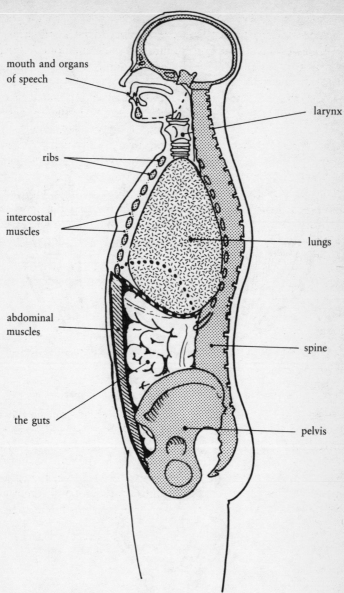

17 **The vocal tract in relation to the torso**

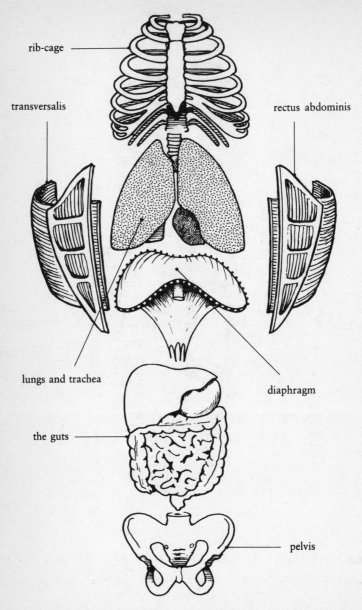

rib-cage

transversalis

rectus abdominis

lungs and trachea

diaphragm

the guts

pelvis

18 Exploded front view of rib-cage, lungs, diaphragm and abdominal muscles

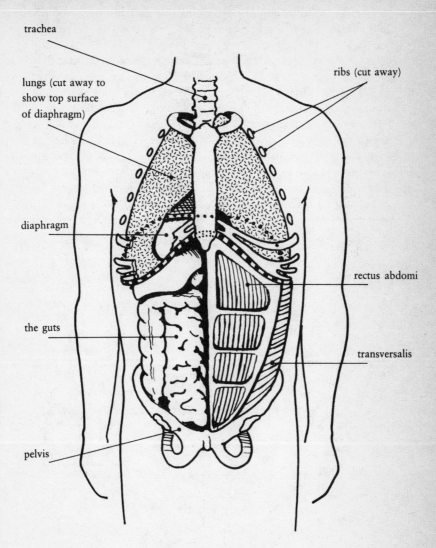

trachea

lungs (cut away to
show top surface
of diaphragm)

ribs (cut away)

diaphragm

rectus abdomi

the guts

transversalis

pelvis

▬▬▬▭▭▭▬ line of attachment between diaphragm and lower rib-cage

• • • • • • • • • • • line to indicate top surface of diaphragm

19 Front view of rib-cage, lungs, diaphragm and abdominal muscles

The vocal cords and the glottis

In the larynx, and largely responsible for its action as a valve, are the vocal cords. Their name can be misleading for they are not really cords at all in the sense of being, as it were, a couple of strings; they are made of muscle and ligament extruding from the inside walls of the larynx. They stretch horizontally and from front to back: in the front they attach to the Adam's apple and at the back to two moveable cartilages called the arytenoid cartilages. When the arytenoids move and rotate, the cords move as well, being helped in this by their own muscle fibres. The action of the cords in moving together and apart can be very rapid, and during phonation, this action converts the airstream into a series of puffs which can be heard as sound. This sound wave, duly resonated, is the voice.

20/21   The larynx

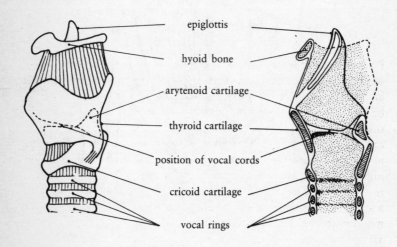

epiglottis

hyoid bone

arytenoid cartilage

thyroid cartilage

position of vocal cords

cricoid cartilage

vocal rings

Side view of larynx   Section through larynx

22/23   **The glottis**

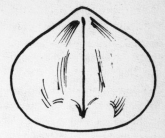

At birth the vocal cords are about 6 mm long for boys and girls. By the time the larynx is fully developed, the cords will be about 30 mm long for a man and about 20 mm for a woman. These drawings are considerably larger than life-size, and show the glottis from above with the cords apart as for inspiration, and closed during phonation

Pitch and volume

Pitch and volume are closely related in ordinary speech. Usually when we speak quietly or normally, we have little need for volume and we also use our lower notes. When we get excited or have to be heard across a larger space than usual we tend to lift the pitch of the voice and also to speak more loudly; hence the idea of 'speaking up'. However, in the theatre, or when addressing a meeting, we do not always want to have to 'speak up' in order to be heard; we might want to use our ordinary conversational pitch, while still reaching the whole audience; we may want to play a character with a low-pitched voice and still be completely audible; conversely, we might wish to play a role in a higher voice-pitch than is usual for us and to be able to express the normal range of emotion without sounding over-loud or hysterical. To use the voice in these ways is probably, for most of us, to make a departure from everyday use which will at first be a little strange. It is in such a case that we begin to need a vocal technique.

In order to be able to understand how we may control pitch and volume independently it may help to consider shortly what happens to make the pitch of the note and what we have to do in order to make it louder or quieter.

The pitch of a note is determined by the number of puffs of air that pass through the glottis in a given time. The more puffs per second, the higher the pitch of the note. The movements of the glottis in making these puffs of air are produced by its intrinsic muscles.

The volume of the sound is directly controlled first by the wish to speak louder or quieter, which produces the appropriate action of the cords, and then by the adjustment of the breath pressure. As the sound becomes louder, the vocal cords present more of a barrier to the breath by staying closed longer between each puff of air (although the puffs are still allowed through at the same number per second for any given note regardless of increase or decrease in breath pressure).

Now let's consider why, when we use the voice in everyday life, there is a tendency to raise the note as the volume is increased.

It is the action of the vocal cords upon the airstream which produces the sound wave; it follows that the airstream must pass between the cords for the sound to be made, and to do this it must be at a sufficient pressure. As the note gets higher, the cords open and close faster, as we have seen, and the space between them becomes shorter and narrower. This makes more of a barrier to the air-flow, and consequently, the higher we speak, the more we tend to increase the breath pressure; the consequence is that we speak more loudly. And so we set up an association of ideas and muscular responses and when we wish to speak more loudly we tend automatically to raise the pitch. The result of this is that we are unaccustomed to using the muscles of the larynx in other patterns of behaviour, and when we try to do so they are at first sluggish and uncertain in their response. They need training, and that is the reason for some of the exercises which follow at the end of this chapter.

Resonance

In order for the sound wave created by the action of the vocal cords on the airstream to have a useful vocal quality the basic note needs to be harmonically enriched, and this happens first of all in the resonators. Our resonators are partially enclosed air-filled spaces in which the original note reverberates, disturbing the air in the cavities and bringing about other reverberations with different frequencies of vibration which are harmonically sympathetic to the original note. This is the process of resonating. As the sound wave, so enriched, leaves the body, it reverberates the air around us, and, according to the size and shape of the space we are in, the quality of the sound is affected. The sound wave loses power the further it gets from the body and the sound gets quieter. The sound is further quietened as the sound wave is absorbed by non-reflecting surfaces. A good deal of the voice is absorbed, for example, by the tissues which line the resonators; more will be absorbed by carpets, upholstery and by the people in the space in which we are speaking.

The resonators

The room

The acoustic quality of the place in which we do our voice practice is important, and it is better not to practise in a 'dead' space where the voice is too quickly absorbed. The better the reflecting qualities of the space the more physical help it is to us in arriving at a good use of the voice. If we speak in a room with good sound-reflecting qualities – say a room which has walls and floors made of glazed tiles, we shall hear the voice as richer, fuller and more brilliant than if we speak in the same room where carpet has replaced the tiles. In fact the acoustic properties of a tiled room may flatter the voice considerably (nearly everyone sings well in the bathroom!) but it is encouraging as well. We shall also notice that each room has its own particular optimum pitch, and that if we speak on that pitch our voice seems to produce a better quality of sound and to need less effort to resonate fully.

On the other hand, if we speak in the open air without any sound-reflecting surfaces around us, the voice seems lifeless and it is hard work to produce any quality of richness in it. Indeed, sometimes the effect upon the actor of working in a poor acoustic environment such as the open air is that he *cannot* produce his voice well and suffers a consequent strain. This is because when we use our voices, especially to address the public in a large space, we are dependent upon the ear, which, as the reflected sound waves enter it, feeds back messages to the brain telling us to do this or that to produce the quality we feel is needed. This is our monitoring process and if it doesn't have enough information – or feedback – to work upon it won't function properly. But don't carry your search for reflecting surfaces to the point where you end up practising in an echo chamber! The sound of the voice should be live and vibrant but undistorted. Perhaps more important than this is that the place where you practise should ideally be somewhere you *enjoy* using the voice.

The mouth and throat

The important voice resonators in the body are linked so the vibrating airstream can enter all of them. Working up from the glottis, the first in the chain, and the most important, are those of the throat and mouth. The throat and mouth are two large resonators coupled together and have almost limitless possibilities of adjustment, a property which the other resonators do not have. Not all resonators work equally well for the enrichment of all notes; but the adjustability of the throat and mouth resonators means that we have it in our power from moment to moment to make them serve the changing note to maximum advantage. We can change the size and shape of these resonators, and so their acoustic properties, by moving the larynx, the tongue, the soft palate, the jaw, the lips and the cheeks; also, the walls of the pharynx itself have elasticity and can change shape to some extent.

The nose

We normally use the nose as a resonator only for the nasal consonants [m, n, ŋ] and for nasalized vowels, if such occur in the language we are speaking – French, Portuguese and Catalan have a fair number, for example. But we can, if we choose, nasalize the whole speech pattern to some extent. The nose is separated from the mouth and the top of the pharynx by the action of the soft palate in lifting to join with the back wall of the throat at the top of the pharynx. When the soft palate is dropped, the airstream passes into the nose.

The sinuses

Connected with the nose by a labyrinthine series of passageways are the sinuses, or head cells. In the cheek bones are the maxillary sinuses which have a small opening apiece directly into the nose; over the eyes are the frontal sinuses; on a level with the eyes but further back in the skull are the sphenoid sinuses; between the sphenoids and the frontal sinuses are the anterior and posterior ethmoid cells.

The function of these sinuses in voice production is much disputed. There is a body of opinion which claims that the airstream may be directed into them and that they may thus be used as true resonators, and by changing the flow of air between the sinuses control of tone and pitch may be exercised. However, the generally accepted opinion is that the sinuses play no appreciable part in resonating the voice and no part at all in determining the pitch.

I believe it is possible that the sinuses may add some qualities to the resonation of the voice when the soft palate is partially dropped and the voice is directed to buzz the head and the mask of the face. The notable falling off in the brighter tones of the voice during a head cold may in part be due to the sinuses having become clogged with mucus, although it is probably mostly due to congestion of the nasal cavity. The theory that the voice is actually produced in the sinuses seems to me to fly in the face of the evidence.

Sensation

We have discussed at some length the actions of the glottis and what goes on in the throat; this has been to help in understanding the processes by which we produce voice. But now we come to begin working the voice and playing around with it to see what we can do, and from now on, except during one exercise which will be explained in due course, all our vocal activity is performed almost as if the larynx and the vocal cords did not exist; for during phonation we should have little or no sensation in that area. We may feel the Adam's apple buzz if we touch the neck at that point during phonation, but inside the throat it is as if everything is quite peaceful. If we feel pinching sensations, strain or roughness at the laryngeal level it is a warning that we are doing something wrong

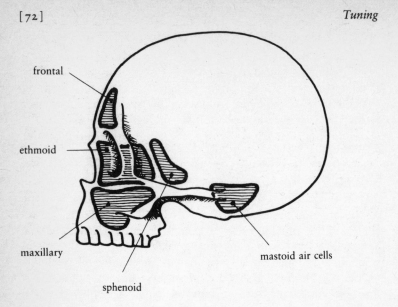

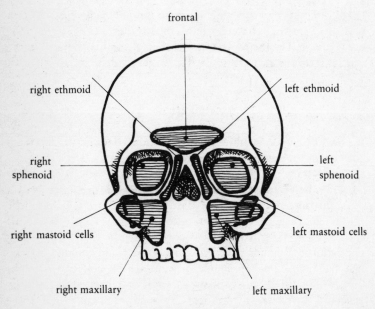

24   The head sinuses

or overworking; at such a moment it is best to stop practice and rest for a while. Never force for a result.

Because here we are concerned with developing various kinds of muscular control and are therefore exercising muscles in an unaccustomed way, we shall find from time to time that various muscles will get tired and may even ache for a while or feel more stretched than usual; this does not necessarily mean that we are doing something wrong; a small ache or tiredness is not to be confused with soreness resulting from damaging use. Nevertheless, if you do begin to ache, stop work for a while. During the whole of your practice, make sure you keep your neck free and maintain your basic good use. You will find this difficult at times, particularly when practising your upper range or using the voice very loudly, but keeping your directions and a good head/neck/back relationship will do more than anything else to help you keep the throat undamaged however hard you are working the voice.

If we are not to have sensation at the laryngeal level while we produce voice, where *are* we to feel things going on? And what will these feelings be like?

This will depend a great deal on what kind of noise you are making, and as we go through the various exercises I shall try to provide a guide as to what sensations you should expect to experience, and those you should not. However, these descriptions will not be complete, for when we change the use of the voice often we experience feelings which are psychological in nature – caused no doubt by use of the muscles, but not measurable as a muscular response. These feelings are highly subjective and individual but certain common patterns do emerge. When the voice is well produced, that is with mechanical efficiency, often the vocalist experiences feelings of relief, euphoria and self-satisfaction. Before the voice is released, but while we are working to release it, it is quite common to have feelings of anxiety, to feel unsure of oneself and even to panic. In this it is rather like learning to ride a bicycle. Soon we become familiar with the differences of use we are practising and they cease to alarm and become enjoyable as we realize we can do more and more with our voice and that we have more effective control over it. And of course, as communicators we have the great joy of realizing that we have more and better means of communication at our disposal.

While we are on the subject of responses to voice change it might be helpful to note that most of the people I have worked with have professed themselves dissatisfied with their voices – why else would they want help with them? – but this hasn't stopped many of them from *feeling* a great reluctance to change the use of the voice from what has been familiar. This reluctance is entirely understandable. Our voice is so intimately a part of us that to change the way we use it seems akin to tampering with our personality: 'What comes out of my mouth as speech is *me* – when I make these strange vocal noises I no longer recognize myself in them – I feel false!' Don't worry! The more you use the new sounds the more you will become used to them. Normally we only use a small part of our vocal potential and it's quite a shock to discover the fullness of it. However, we don't stop being ourselves because we use more of our capabilities.

Sometimes the actor gets round the problem of accepting a new voice use by putting it at the service of the characters he plays and doesn't use it in ordinary life. There's nothing wrong with this, and how we use our voice must be a matter of choice; and certainly an actor who continually demonstrates the full power and range of his voice during ordinary conversation is going to make tedious company. But if our habitual voice use is mechanically poor – back-to-front breathing, forcing from the throat or whatever our bad habit is, then by using it during ordinary everyday life we only reinforce that bad habit and this will make it so much more difficult to free the voice when we come to use it in public. The more we use a physical skill, the more accessible to use it becomes. In this way, using the voice well in ordinary life is a great help in our training.

The physical feelings we experience when we use our voice can be more easily described and are likely to be similar for most voice users. If you hum with your lips closed, for example, you are bound to feel a buzz in your nose because the voice is resonating there and the airstream is passing through the nose on its way out. You may also, by thinking of directing the airstream against the lips while you are humming, feel the buzz there. And if you put a hand on the top of your head and continue this buzz, you will probably feel a vibration, and if you do not, by directing the voice to buzz in that area, you will find after a bit of trial and error that it does. These are examples of common and basic sensations associated with

humming; every difference of voice use has its own series of
sensations and I shall describe the more usual of these as the need
arises.

Exercises

Introduction

As you begin the exercises all of your attention will probably be on
how you are doing things physically. Later on, as you gain confi-
dence in the responsiveness of your voice and increased familiarity
with the work procedures frees your attention to deal with other
things, *make sure* you give yourself a communicative intention for
the sounds you are making. They may not be words yet, but you
can treat them as though they are, and this method, while leaving
you free to get the voice working well without having to worry
about the complications of the full articulatory process, will provide
a bridge into it when you begin working with the consonants. If
this sounds as though I am saying that on no account should you
speak words while you are working through this part of the method,
of course I'm not. Try to apply what you have found out about the
way your voice works, in fully articulate speech, as often as you
can. Do this casually, in conversation; do it carefully working on
texts; explore it for all it's worth.

The murmur

This exercise should first be performed on the floor with your knees
up and your head on the books, and can form a continuation of the
jaw-release work. It helps if the floor is made of wood; it will vibrate
in sympathy with your voice and the feeling of those vibrations can
be a great encouragement.

Allow the jaw to be open, but the lips closed as for [m]. The tongue
is flat in the mouth as if you were preparing to say 'Ah'.

Without disturbing your breathing pattern, use the out-breath to
make voice on a descending note from the middle of your
comfortable range.

Direct the resonance fully into the nose and closed mouth.

You should feel the nose and lips vibrate. It is as if you are sighing, for at this point you are not doing much to restrain the breath-flow, so you will find the voice tails off as you get to the lowest notes.

While you are making this sound, let it be at whatever volume is comfortable.

Encourage the vibrations to fill not only your head but your chest as well.

If you feel with your hands you should be able to sense the vibrations in your skull, breast bone, and in the rib-cage, both at the front and back.

Keeping the back of the mouth well open – and for this to happen your jaw must be free – allow your starting point for the sliding note to be a little higher each time.

But make sure you don't tense the tongue while you are doing this. If you do, the note will feel bottled-up in the throat instead of being free to come into the mask of the face.

Now begin to loosen the lips into a close [b/v] shape and direct the voice-stream towards the front of the hard palate; as you do so, the voice will sound less and less nasal but still have a firm and vibrant richness. Think of making as much space as you can in the back of the mouth, but leave the tongue-root quite free and untensed.

The tongue-root
The tongue-root should be kept as free and untensed as possible the whole time the voice is being used. The tongue is a supple organ and can change its shape in a variety of directions simultaneously, but too much contraction at the root will produce a throaty, sometimes half-strangled sound which is unpleasant and doesn't travel far since it is mostly absorbed by the tissue of the tongue and pharynx and so becomes muffled.

You can check whether or not the tongue-root is over-tensed during speech by putting a finger under your jaw in the soft part between the bone and in front of the neck; if there is a pushing against your finger, stop, inhibit the tongue from tightening, and start again.

Often the tongue-root tenses because there is something wrong with the breathing: for example gaspers nearly always contract the tongue-root when they take a breath. So check your breathing. Are you collapsing and pulling down? Are you pushing forward with the lower part of the abdomen as you speak? The pressure of the abdominal muscles is fairly light during performance of the Murmur, upward in the direction of the breath-flow and inward towards the back bone. As in the breathing exercises, make sure you don't lose length. If your breathing goes astray, you may try to energize the voice from the throat and thereby over-tense the tongue; so make sure, even for these very simple quiet sounds, that you are supporting the voice properly with your breath.

Be patient about correcting the tendency to over-tighten the tongue-root. People who have this tendency sometimes take quite a long time to avoid it. But the more you have worked through the body work of the first section, the easier you will find it to make any of these physical adjustments. This correction, for example, relies on your ability to inhibit the first response: the Stop–Release procedure.

The Whispered 'Ah' is a good exercise for helping to release the tongue-root. Another takes the Whispered 'Ah' as its starting point and continues the 'Ah' into 'EE' [ɑ:→i:]. Feel with a finger to see if the tongue wants to tighten or push as you move from [ɑ:] to [i:] joining the two sounds to form an extended diphthong. You should find it possible to move the body of the tongue as you change vowels without any push in the root. Practise until you can do this comfortably and then put voice to the vowels. Then use the other vowels in various combinations and keep the tongue-root free.

Body buzz

This is a direct continuation of the first exercise.

The jaw is open and the lips rounded as for [u:]. Using this vowel to begin with, keeping the volume fairly quiet at first and always even, whatever the note, glide from a high note down to your lowest note in the speaking register.

Don't worry if the top notes are falsetto to begin with, but try to keep the transition from falsetto to normal voice smooth and without a pitch-break. When you arrive at the lower notes you should find that they have a rich speaking quality. Women sometimes keep the voice in the head register and often don't bring the note down to the real bottom of their range.

If in doubt, prolong one of the low notes and then turn it into a spoken word; if you find there is an abrupt change of quality or a break in the voice when you do this, you have held on to the head voice.

Eventually this exercise should be performed entirely in a comfortable speaking range, which integrates the top part of the voice with the bottom. This is what you are aiming for, but take things gently. The more you manage to open up the mouth/throat resonator the better the quality will become and the less you will be likely to hang on to the thin unenriched falsetto quality. (See also Pitch-Break: Registers, pp. 92–100.)

Slide the note – slowly – down the scale but don't try to make it last for ever; and while you are doing it, listen, and try to be aware of the quality of the sound and your physical sensations.

The voice should be firm and clear, unsmudged by extra, unresonated breath. You should feel a light buzz in the hard palate and in the teeth at the front of the mouth.

You should also feel the action of your abdominal muscles as they support the breath. Since you are keeping the volume constant, your rib-cage will narrow at an even rate and you might feel as though it is being kept open or restrained from the collapse of a sigh by the pull of the rib muscles.

If you spread your arms on the floor, you may feel it vibrate. When the voice is going well, you should feel as if all of you is vibrating: hands, head, chest, back, stomach, legs . . . all of you, as if there is an aura of voice round your body. This is accompanied by a feeling of ease and expansiveness as you release the various joints and muscles.

When you begin to feel that the voice is working in every part of you, change the vowel to [i:].

Again, keep the sound focused on the hard palate, and to help this don't let your lips spread too wide nor the teeth be far apart. The opening of the front of the mouth hardly ever needs to be great, and if it is overdone can dissipate the resonance; much more important are the opening within the mouth, the release of the jaw and the lifting of the soft palate.

As you open the back of the mouth there is a stretching sensation as the palate lifts; it is almost as though you are trying to yawn without showing it.

When you have worked [u:] and [i:] move on to [ɔ:] and [e:] and [ɑ:] (as in 'm*o*re, br*ea*d, Ch*a*rles', but with *all* the vowels lengthened).

The next stage is to repeat the process and reverse the tune moving the note from low to high, still keeping the volume even.

Make sure you don't tighten the neck as you reach the high notes, and inhibit the tendency to push at them or force them with a lot of volume. On the other hand, don't lose support as you raise the pitch.

An alternative form for starting this exercise is to establish the body buzz on one held note which you find comfortable, probably somewhere in your lower range. When the buzz is going well and you feel full of voice, gradually begin moving the note up and down, keeping the volume constant and carrying as much of the richness of the sound as you can from note to note.

As you have been performing these exercises you have been working on pitch and volume control, to some extent you have been directing the resonance placing of the voice, and you have begun to use the breath support. All the basic voice-developing elements are here. The Murmur and the Body Buzz can now be further developed into speech and singing, as long as the fundamental voice sound is properly made.

Problems

It is likely, however, that the exercises have posed some problems. These will vary from person to person, and some fortunate people may indeed have found that they have experienced no problems at all, in which case they are ready for more athletic things. But before we go on to the more virtuoso exercises and since it is important to get the basic voice sound working well, we shall deal with the more common problems which doing these exercises may have revealed. They will fall into three categories:

Breathing
Converting the breath into voice
Directing the placing of the sound.

All the problems are muscular, but some of the muscles used in producing the sound are so hidden, and we have so little apparent direct contact with them, that it doesn't help to talk about them and we fall back on the use of imagery instead.

Not all images work for all people and often you will have to invent your own; however, between observation, experiment, description of sensation and imagery, we shall arrive at an understanding of what we are trying to do.

The breathy voice

What do we mean by 'breathy voice'? and is it necessarily a bad thing? A voice may be said to be breathy if during speech or song so much air is coming out of the mouth so fast that a reasonably long phrase cannot be sustained. Also, there is a quality of sound special to this type of production: a grainy quality in the note, a huskiness, and sometimes you can quite clearly hear a susurration of unresonant breath around the note. Often people find a breathy voice, particularly the husky variety, attractive, and there's no particular reason to abolish the quality if it doesn't get in the way of your communication. But there is every reason to have it under control. Because the breathy voice uses up your air at a prodigal rate, it is often difficult to make it serve the needs of the stage performance, although it can work well with microphones. Some speakers who are normally breathy make an automatic adjustment as soon as they need to use the voice more loudly or resonantly than usual. But if you have breathy voice production and do not make such an adjustment, you could well find yourself in trouble and suffering from voice loss when you come to make more volume. As you pump more and more air through the throat to support the rise in volume you begin to gasp, and heave in the upper chest in order to get enough breath to last the phrase out. And as all this unvoiced breath, at great pressure, passes between the cords it has an abrasive effect upon them and you begin to get a sore throat. Then everything gets worse and you have to force to tune the higher notes and your effective range becomes smaller and smaller.

What causes breathy voice?

Obviously it must be something which is going wrong with the breath management, and the most usual thing is pulling down during the out-breath. This leads to a collapse, even though it may seem quite a small one, and then it is as if a sigh is creeping into the voice. So the first thing to check is the breathing; look to see if the collar bones or the breast bone are pulling down. Often, just by making sure that there is no such pulling down, the breath support starts working properly and the breathy quality disappears from the voice.

Breathiness may also come about because the cords have been badly used over a long period and now find great difficulty in tuning the breath-stream. In this case there is usually a rougher quality to the sound and great difficulty is experienced with the high notes. If your voice has this kind of quality and does not improve as you do the exercises, it is advisable to see a laryngologist and have the cords looked at – it is possible that you have been developing nodules on them. If it turns out that you have got nodules, and if they are large enough, some laryngologists advise surgery to remove them. This should be an absolutely last resort. You have to find out *why* the nodules are there. If, as is usual, particularly among people who use their voices consistently at considerable volume – actors, singers, public speakers – the nodules have been caused by bad use of the voice, there is every chance that changing the bad use for good use will so improve the basic condition that the nodules will go away without surgery. But if you have these unpleasant growths, you must be very sensible about how you use the voice while the situation is mending: you should certainly not sing or shout, you shouldn't smoke, and above all you should work on your basic body use. I have not yet come across a case of nodules on the cords which was not accompanied by a poor head/neck relationship. I don't say that they don't exist apart from this condition, only that I have not yet met them. But in any event, before allowing surgery, get a second opinion.

How do you get rid of breathiness?

The finger test

One of the oldest methods is to hold a finger across the lips and refuse to let air blow on it as you voice the various vowels at various pitches and volumes. You have to be careful not to hold your breath while you are doing this; if you do, the voice will sound very odd indeed and as if you are about to explode. What you are trying to do is manage the breath, not stop it. As you are making the vowel you will experience the following:

1 Slight warmth on the finger – but no draught!

2 A stretching inside the back of the mouth.

3 A want to pull the tongue back and tense it. Not everyone will feel this; if you do it is to be resisted.

4 A pressure, as if from within the rib-cage, against the ribs; this is most felt at the sides of the cage, but you will also feel it as a forward pressure between the costal arch. Allow this to happen, but don't actively push the ribs out, there is no need.

5 Because you have opened the mouth/throat resonator more, the voice will sound richer, and perhaps lower – though this is likely to be more because the lower harmonics are being heard rather than because you have actually put the base tone lower.

Try holding a note and then a higher note, the fullness of the resonance should stay with you through the whole of the lower and middle range of the voice.

This fullness of resonance often comes as a shock to breathy speakers who may never have heard the voice working at something near its proper potential because habitually they have kept the mouth/throat resonator fairly closed, often keeping the tongue high and occupying a great deal of mouth space. This exercise will remedy that state of things – but do keep the tongue-root free and untensed.

Glottic popping

There is another way of tackling breathiness, and in this exercise we have to be conscious of what we are doing with the glottis. Breathiness is caused by, or results in, an inadequate closure of the glottis during phonation. Sometimes it is difficult for the speaker to hear that his voice is breathy and even more difficult to sense what is happening, or not happening, to make it so. However, if despite the foregoing work that telltale draught still blows on your fingers when you make the vowel, this is an exercise which will help. Each stage is as important as any other.

1 Go through the Whispered 'Ah'.

2 Keeping the neck and tongue-root free stop the breath in your throat while still gently applying pressure on the breath with the abdominal muscles. When this is done, the glottis closes and you feel it as an obstruction to the breath.

3 Release the throat. There will be a small popping unvoiced explosion as the cords part and let the breath through. This will probably be followed by a sigh, but don't collapse.

4 Repeat this sequence, but as soon as the glottic pop is made, close off the air supply again in the same way; release and close, release and close, until you have a fairly rapid series of pops going – as lightly as possible, for you do this with the minimum expenditure of breath. You should not now feel that draught on your finger. Instead, because you are using up the air very slowly, you will feel as though you have too much of it and want to expel it in a sigh every now and then. You will also notice your abdominal muscles working with a fair degree of tonus, and your ribs staying open longer.

5 Now you have some sense of where the sound begins and can take the process into voice. But here you have to be careful not to overdo things. You have to avoid the collapse and the

over-use of air which goes with it, but you don't want the opposite extreme of a locked throat, nor the sensation of holding the voice there and pushing with the breath as though you are about to burp. Release the pop and at the same time vocalize, joining the vowels [ɑ:] and [i:]. It's as if the pop is the first release of the cords in the rapid series of closures and releases they perform to make the sound. Keep the pop as light as possible, but maintain the feeling of the air being sounded at the glottic level and don't let the breath-stream become a sigh once you have started voicing. Try a few swoops up and down your medium pitch-range, extending the [ɑ:→i:] into a long diphthong. At first you probably won't be able to manage very long sounds without wanting to collapse, but as you practise you should be able to sustain the note more and more.

6 For speaking purposes you have to make sure that you do not stay with what probably sounds like a very over-produced noise, and you have to be able to make the tuned sound without the sense that you are performing complicated oral gymnastics and be able to link it easily with normal speech.

Make [w] or a close [u] before the [ɑ:→i:]. As you shape the first part of this threefold sound, again think of the glottis closing as for the pop, and release the sound from that point. Now gradually eliminate the pop sound, but keep the solidly resonated quality of the [uɑi]. Now, still keeping the quality of the sound the same, put an [h] before the vowels. The [h] will be very slight and hardly there at all, but you will have eased the 'bottled' feeling in the vowels.

Now you are no longer starting the sound with a glottic explosion but with an unvoiced consonant. This means you are allowing a little unresonated air through the glottis, and then tuning the breath-stream, which more nearly approximates to the processes of ordinary speech. It is more difficult to maintain the tuning of the vowel when it follows an unvoiced consonant than when it is preceded by a voiced sound. If you can achieve [h] plus vowel, try [f] plus vowel. If you can do this and maintain the firm resonation of the vowel you have solved the problem.

7 However, there is still one more important stage to this exercise.

Now you have to maintain the clear, unbreathy resonance while you shift your attention away from the throat and try to use the sound to buzz the body, as if it fills you, rising through your whole length. And now is the time to play with the sound, letting it be breathy one moment and not the next.

Don't be in too much of a hurry as you do this work. You may find that merely understanding how to control the breath-to-resonance process helps you to achieve a great deal of control almost immediately. You may not. You might have to work at it for many hours spread over three or four weeks. As you are working remember that the technique of inhibiting the first, habitual, response is invaluable; it will help you not to try too hard and not to get into a state of tension which destroys your chances of producing in the end the fully resonant voice with ease and freedom.

The glottic attack

We have used the Glottic Pop to help get round the problem of breathiness, but there are those speakers who consistently use such an explosion, in an exaggerated and audible form, to begin any word that starts with a vowel. It is called the glottic shock. If it is consistently part of the speech pattern it needs some attention because it is symptomatic of something going wrong. Often it is the result of a nervousness in the speaker which produces such a state of tension in the breathing muscles and the larynx that in order to speak he has to break a spasm, or lock, in the system. We *hear* the tension being partly released in the glottic shock before vowels; but even so, there is still too much tension remaining in the speaker to allow proper voice control, and this tension will probably not confine itself to the ribs, abdominal muscles and larynx, but affect the throat, jaw, tongue and neck as well. The overall effect it produces in speech is staccato, with no connecting flow between the various sounds; it's as if you can hear the voice being held back. The quality of resonance in a speaker who uses the glottic shock a great deal is often thin and harsh, and the voice doesn't sound as if it belongs to the whole body. The remedy for this is firstly to inhibit the spasmodic approach to speaking by making sure the basic use of the body is good, great attention being given to the neck release.

We want to establish a smooth flow of resonated air without undue tightening of any of the muscles involved. It is the moment just before we make the sound which is of great importance here. Before, during and after making the sound we must keep the neck free and inhibit the first spasm as we go to speak. I find working from a sighed [m] as in the Murmur a great help in making a smooth connection of breath to sound. It helps, too, to think during practice that all of the speech-stream is carried on a silent [h]. The latter stages of the Glottic Pop, those where the attention is on re-establishing the breath-to-voice link, are helpful. But the basic cure must be found in developing an ability to inhibit the spasm of the locked breath-stream. It will mean a lot of careful self-monitoring to get the conscious control working, but it's well worth it. You will feel a sense of completeness and relief when speaking without the spasm, and the voice will be enriched a great deal.

Nasality and nasal resonance: the function of the soft palate

Nasality is a common problem among speakers; it occurs when the breath-stream is permanently directed into the nose – it is nasal resonance when you don't want it. Voices which are coloured with nasality are often thin, metallic or reedy in quality; in some cases they sound a bit duck-like. Sometimes people talk about the voice being nasal when describing the sound of someone with a bad cold. They call that sound nasal because they are aware of the nose when they listen to it, but actually what they are hearing is a lack of nasal resonance because the nose is so stuffed-up that the airstream can hardly get into the nasal cavity to resonate – or if it can get in at the back it can't come out again at the front through the nostrils. There is another quality of nasality which occurs when most of the breath-stream is directed into the nose and resonates fully there – it is a kind of rich honking sound, more like a fog-horn than a duck. This sound has great carrying power, even though it can be somewhat muffled in character, and there are methods of singing based on placing the voice so that this honk is fully exploited. However, for the actor or public speaker both forms of nasality though they may from time to time be useful – especially to the actor in his characterization work – are too limiting to become a permanent or usual mode of voice use.

    In controlling the nasal quality of the voice we have to be able to direct the action of the soft palate. If you feel back across the roof of the mouth with the tip of your tongue you will feel that at a certain point the hard palate continues into a softer substance. This is the soft palate and it is muscle. For some people the control of this muscle is a matter of great difficulty. Breathy speakers as well as nasal speakers often find themselves confused when it comes to using the soft palate and they feel they can have no direct control over it. But patient work will yield the necessary results. And control of the soft palate is very necessary. It is the soft palate which helps control the direction of the airstream. If it is dropped away from the back wall of the pharynx during expiration, air enters the nose; when it is raised and seals with the wall of the pharynx, it prevents air getting into the nose. It is highly flexible, and according to the amount it is raised and stretched it can produce many changes of quality in the resonance.

Exercises for the soft palate

The nasal consonants

The sounds for which we need to use the nose directly as a resonator are the nasal consonants [m, n, ŋ]. For these the palate must be well-dropped so that the airstream can pass unobstructed into the nose. It is a curious fact that those who employ the duck-like nasality very rarely have good nasal resonance for the nasal consonants; that is because the palate is always kept in the same position, slightly dropped, so there is an overall uniformity of resonance. When the nasal consonants are produced with the maximum resonation the palate is well dropped. So the first of the exercises for getting the soft palate under control is to practise the nasal consonants with a fullness of resonance in the mask of the face – until your lips and nose tingle.

[m]

Keep the lips closed and the jaw open, the tongue flat as for [ɑ:]; direct the resonating breath-stream into the nose and against the lips. The resonance should make the nose, lips, cheeks and the top of your skull vibrate.

[n]

The lips are apart, the tongue-tip lifted to touch the hard palate just behind the teeth.

Make the most space possible in the mouth without tensing the
tongue-root.

Direct the voice-stream into the nose and against the tongue-tip,
which should tingle; you will feel the resonance buzz in the nose
and cheeks and the top of the skull.

[ŋ] (as in sing)

For this sound the back of the tongue rises to meet the dropped soft
palate so that the resonating space is the throat and nose (the throat,
of course, resonates for all of the voiced sounds); you will still feel
the vibrations in the nose, cheeks and skull.

When you have got the nasal consonants resonating well, try adding
a vowel – [ɑ:] is probably best – after the consonant.

But think of the vowel as opening the back of the mouth even more
– it is almost as though you have to stretch back in the mouth to
make the vowel. This should cause the soft palate to spring
upward to seal off the nose. If the nasality persists, try the
following exercises.

The cold cure

This is not a cure for the cold, but speaking as if you have one, as
if the nose is so stuffed-up that no air can get into it. If you can
produce this effect you are probably lifting the soft palate, and
keeping it raised.

To test whether the palate is lifted pinch your nostrils together:
there should be no feeling that you are stopping any of the air-
flow because all of the air should be coming out of your mouth:
there should be no change in the resonance either.

The next stage is to allow the nasal consonants back into the nose.
Use the sequence:

[ɑ:, ɑ:m, ɑ:mɑ:, ɑ:mɑ:m]

and then substitute the other vowels and, in turn, the other nasal
consonants.

For [ɑ:] you should sound as though you have a bad cold; and test
that no air is coming through the nose. You should feel a great
stretching in the roof of your mouth at the back. Because you are

enlarging the mouth/throat resonator your voice will sound a bit hollow to you.

As you move from [ɑː] to [m] you close the lips and divert the airstream into the nose, as if it is going straight up into the skull.

To go back to the open vowel, from [m] to [ɑː], you open the lips, and as you do so, think of enlarging the cavity at the back of the mouth even more. Test to see if any air comes down the nose.

Now play with the nasal sounds and the vowels, rapidly moving from nasal to non-nasal sound; repeat this on different notes.

Be careful to keep the jaw free. The opening between the teeth need not be great but the opening in the back of the mouth must be.

This may make you want to yawn – do, it's good exercise! It might also make you want to pull the jaw back – don't; that way lies a closed throat and tight tongue.

Yawning

Because with nasality the back of the mouth isn't open *enough*, try the *exaggerated* opening which comes with yawning.

But instead of opening the mouth at the front fully, keep the teeth fairly close together as you yawn, and round the lips so that you are saying [uː].

Keeping some of the yawn feeling, follow the [uː] with [m], then back to [uː] and build up a sequence. Then use the other vowels in the same way; then the other nasal consonants.

After you have begun to lift and drop the soft palate at will, you still need to balance the overall resonance, otherwise you might end up hooting the vowels and honking the nasal consonants, for we have adopted exaggerated uses just in order to get the palate moving. So at this stage, go back to the first two exercises in Tuning (pp. 75–9) and work through them again, paying particular attention to buzzing the hard palate, particularly the front of it. This will restore a sense that the nose is working. As you vibrate the hard palate, the vibration is transmitted through it to the nasal cavity above and causes some vibration of the air inside it, even if the soft palate is sealing off the nose from the direct flow of the airstream.

It is not nasal resonance proper, as for the nasal consonants, nor is it nasality in any of its quacking or honking forms. It is a bright overtone to the voice and helps it sound firmly and richly resonant.

Lack of nasal resonance

When people talk as if they have a permanent cold it is probable that there is in fact some congestion in the nasal area. It could be that the adenoids are enlarged, and if so they will need medical treatment. Sometimes the nasal passages are blocked, or partly so, by a distortion of the septum, which is the central divider of the nose; often this can be corrected by surgery, and if the distortion is so severe that very little air can be made to issue from the nostrils it is probably a good thing to have it attended to. Mucus may act as a congestant and affect resonation, and so may allergies, hay-fever and the like. Sometimes these can be alleviated by good voice and body use, but if the stuffed-up feeling persists and there is chronic inflammation of the tissues in the nose you should consult a doctor. (I have found that homoeopathic doctors have often produced the best results with these conditions.)

However, lack of nasal resonance can also be a residue of conditions which prevailed in childhood but are no longer in force. Many a child takes to mouth-breathing because it has a permanently runny nose, for example; sometimes the mouth-breathing will persist into adult life when the runny nose has long dried up; as a consequence, the palate becomes inert and the airstream is always directed into the mouth. Some regional speech patterns, usually urban and industrial, have almost no nasal resonance and this persists even when the speaker is no longer in other ways employing the regional speech.

For those who *can* pass air through the nose, but hardly ever do, one helpful thing is to make sure that they normally breathe through the nose when they are not speaking. For the rest, the exercises on nasal resonance above should suffice to get the nose working. In addition, much humming should be practised.

Too high or too low?

Everyone has a predisposition to speak within a certain part of their total pitch-range, mostly in the middle of the voice, experiencing little difficulty in taking the note up or down as occasion demands.

Some people, however, are inclined to favour one end of their pitch-range and not use the rest of it at all. This tends to make the voice sound if not monotonous at least predictable and robs the speaker not only of his range of note but also of a good part of his expressive range. The favouring of one extremity or other of the pitch-range can also lead to poor resonation: voices which get stuck in the bass notes often sound gruff, throaty and muffled, while voices which stick to the higher notes sound shrill and thin.

When the voice is used over its whole range, the top fills out, the bottom becomes clearer, and the listener has no sense of listening to a voice which is so constrained that it seems as if the speaker can't go up past a certain note – or down, as the case may be.

Exercises for finding your middle pitch

Working with a piano, if you can, try to find out what your effective range is – effective in the sense that the voice retains its fullness of resonance and volume.

Take a short phrase which begins with a vowel and sing it on the middle note of that range, whatever it happens to be.

Then sing the opening vowel of the phrase on that note and speak the rest of the phrase.

Try this with statements and questions so that the phrase has a rise and fall from the middle note:

> [ɑ:] . . . . <u>ah</u> there you are!
> [ɑ:] . . . . <u>are</u> you going out?

If you are accustomed to speaking with the voice permanently pitched down, repeat the process, but gradually, a semitone at a time, lift the starting note.

If you are inclined to pitch the voice very high for normal speech, repeat the process but go down a semitone at a time.

While you are speaking from the new note it is important to ensure that the speaking tune *is* a speaking tune and not some over-musical distortion of it, so you must keep the motivation communicative and not merely 'I am doing my exercises'.

Gradually you should be able to bring the speaking pitch towards the true middle of the voice without losing the availability of the notes you have habitually been using.

While you are doing this exercise, keep the resonance full.

The pitch-break: registers

The pitch-break is a sudden change from the normal adult speaking voice into falsetto or thin head voice; or, in women especially, it can take the form of a sudden breaking plunge into chest voice. Very few speakers normally experience pitch-breaks, but at moments of high stress (pain, crying, laughing, etc.) they can happen to anyone and be accepted as a natural concomitant of the emotion. If they occur during ordinary speech they can be quite an embarrassment and produce unwanted comic effects. Then, too, they are a sign that somewhere things are going wrong.

In order to understand how the pitch-break occurs and how to avoid it, it will be as well at this point to consider some of the differences between male and female voices, particularly in the question of the registers of the voice. Since here we are principally concerned with the speaking voice, a few simple observations will suffice.*

The first register of the voice is also called the chest voice, or the monophase register. It is the lowest of the registers. Most of the adult male voice range lies within it and so does the lowest part of the female range. There is, generally, an overlap where the lowest notes of the female range and the highest notes of the male range – while still in this register – coincide.

The second register is also called head voice in women and falsetto in men and is otherwise known as the biphase register. It contains the highest part of the adult male voice, the full range of the child's voice in both sexes before puberty, and the major part of the adult female voice.

---

*For a neurological description I refer the reader to Raoul Husson's *Le Chant* (Presses Universitaires, Paris 1962). For a description of the muscular processes in producing the various registers, Vennard's *Singing – The Mechanism and the Technic* (Fischer, New York, 1967) may prove useful, and this work together with *Singing – The Physical Nature of the Vocal Organ* by Husler and Rodd-Marling (Hutchinson, London, 1976) seem to me brilliantly to cover the uses and application of register work in singing.

These two registers are sometimes given other names, and other registers in the female voice are variously described, but for our purposes the first two registers are the important ones as the whole of the speaking voice range for men and women lies within them.

The pitch-break in men usually occurs towards the top of the speaking range, and in women usually towards the bottom of the speaking range. It happens when moving from one register to another – but only when the laryngeal muscles are in a poor state of use – or are not sufficiently developed. Normally the movement between the first and second registers should occur so smoothly that the listener is unaware of any transition as the top voice merges into the lower voice, the chest voice into head voice. Overall, the voice quality for both sexes should be firm and solid, brighter in the top of the speaking range (but not piercing or strident), fuller and richer towards the bottom, with both qualities being happily mixed through the large middle range of the voice.

Having said that this 'should' be so, I mean of course in general use. It is not a question of aesthetics but of vocal health. The actor may choose to use pitch-breaks – or any other vocal effect – in the short term or as part of a characterization, but any such habitual misuse will bring about a decay in the working relationship of the laryngeal muscles together with a progressive deterioration in the control of the voice.

When no great range of inflexion is called for, women generally speak in the first register, or chest voice. However, since the major part of their vocal range lies above the first register they more frequently move into the second register or head voice than men. This is not always the case. I have known cases of women who, while able to use the chest voice for singing, have had an antipathy to using it for speaking and have confined themselves to head voice; the speaking voice which is so confined tends to sound ethereal and immature – or merely sharply strident.

Actresses, particularly when they sing without adequate training, often feel themselves to be most secure in the chest voice and, for the sake of continuing in that feeling of security, sometimes push the chest voice up past its easy natural range. This is not the same as merging the chest voice into the head voice – indeed with such voices there is often no head quality at all; the upper notes sound forced or 'belted'. Dramatically this can be quite thrilling at times, the sense of vocal struggle lending considerable emotional intensity to the singing: 'Will she or won't she reach the top note?' However, prolonged use of the 'belting' voice leads inevitably to a coarsening of the overall vocal quality and places a considerable strain on the laryngeal musculature. When the chest voice is pushed up as a matter of habit in speaking it sounds constrained, held down. It's an uncomfortable sound to listen to for any length of time and the throat tensions which accompany it often transmit themselves to the audience – rather as when an actor needs to cough and doesn't; the audience will do it for him, as it were.

Whether the speaking voice is constrained to head voice or chest the problem is the same: a dysfunction of the laryngeal musculature which is keeping the voice from moving easily between the registers; this same dysfunction is likely to provoke unwanted pitch-breaks as well. What to do about putting this state of things right we shall come to at the end of this section.

With male voices the problems are the same but show themselves a little differently. The male voice is more likely to break towards the top of the range. Men are less likely to 'belt' perhaps, but even so, often the listener is aware that the quality which comes from a free top to the voice is missing and the actor, speaking or singing, may be pushing for high notes and sounding uncomfortable. In such a case the actor will almost certainly be experiencing considerable discomfort; his throat will begin to ache and his tongue-root feel squeezed with tension. The whole effect is of a lack of space inside the throat, and this is precisely what is happening.

In setting about curing the pitch-break, as in working to extend the top or bottom of the vocal range, you are seeking to integrate the first two registers, so that you can pass smoothly from one to the other. Several things are involved here but we can summarize as follows:

The breath support must be adequate

The throat must remain open with no feeling of tension at larynx or tongue-root level

The muscular response of the larynx and palate must be adequate and

Acute and accurate aural and sensory appreciation must be developed.

The breath support is dealt with in other exercises, but often the pitch-breaker, or the 'belter', 'reverses' the breathing, pushing outward with the lower abdominal muscles and causing unhelpful pressures and pulls on the throat; this must be put right if the throat is to be free to open.

Usually pitch-breakers have the mouth/throat resonator closed up in some way: the larynx is too high in the throat at the moment the break occurs, or the tongue is pushing back into the pharynx too much; usually, too, the action of the soft palate is faulty, it is insufficiently lifted, and as a consequence often nasality is heard as well. So the mouth/throat resonator needs to be kept well open, and to help this to happen, think of directing the voice up the back wall of the throat and across the roof of the mouth, which you think of being as arched as possible.

This is where the sensory perception and aural awareness are important. You need to be aware of what is happening to your tongue and the palate. You may find the tongue immediately retracting, beginning to tighten into the back of the mouth. This reflex, if it occurs, needs to be inhibited and it's no good trying to stop it by imposing another tension on the tongue and jamming it flat in the floor of the mouth. You must stop, and then allow the arching of the palate and the opening of the throat gently and gradually. In this it helps if your neck is free and a good head/neck relationship is maintained. Often, in any case, the problem will have begun with a collapse of the head/neck relationship; squashing the cervical vertebrae by pulling the head back results in many different kinds of maladjustment between the larynx, breath-stream and resonators and it may be this which is robbing you of the necessary space inside the throat. Keep the jaw free.

If you are not used to arching the palate you will feel an upward pull in it as you perform the exercise; this is a useful indication that things are working well.

Exercises for the pitch-break

The glide: stage 1

This is designed to eliminate the pitch-break and, with slow and careful practice over a lengthy period, to help increase the effective range of the voice. At no stage should the glide be pushed or forced.

On a vowel [u:] first, then [ɑ:], then [i:] make very slow downward glides.

Keep the support working and the sound full and firm at a constant medium volume.

Use a finger to check there is no unnecessary airspill.

The note you start from should be comfortable and in the second register (falsetto for men and head register for women).

Direct the voice as described, keeping the mouth/throat resonator well open.

The glide ends on a comfortable low note in the first or chest register.

At a certain point you will find you want to break from the second register into first (chest register);

At this point try to 'rest' on the break note; you will find this difficult and what is more likely to happen is that you will pass from second to first register without a noticeable break.

You will probably also feel that your throat is wide open as you do this, particularly the back of the throat; you will also feel an unaccustomed pull upward on the soft palate.

As you pass over the break, continue to the comfortable bottom of your range.

The break may continue for a while, but very soon you should find the muscles stabilizing their relationship and not collapsing at the break point. Effectively you have begun to establish control.

Male pitch-breakers are often reluctant to begin from the falsetto because they regard it as the enemy – as if it is the falsetto itself which is to be eliminated. Not so. The true falsetto despite the implications of its name ('false voice') is a very necessary component of the adult voice; if it is missing a great deal of the 'ring' and 'brightness' of the voice disappears, together with some of the top range. However, there are two kinds of falsetto: one is breathy in quality and not to be encouraged because it is produced by a failure of support in the breathing and a poor functioning of some of the laryngeal muscles and the vocal cords; the other kind of falsetto is firmer, quite solid and unbreathy in character and is part of all well developed adult male voices.* This falsetto should be encouraged for the qualities it can bring to the whole voice as well as possibly for use by itself; it is produced by a different kind of muscular activity altogether from the breathy falsetto and calls for well-supported breathing and an action of the laryngeal muscles which is helpful in developing a full quality of voice in the top range.

Occasionally, prolonged misuse will produce a condition in which women seem incapable of producing any head notes. The most common misuse associated with this condition is pulling down in the chest (often seen in depression of the breast bone during out-breath, a slumping of the shoulders and a sagging of the belly). A woman given to such misuse will very likely find that as she tries to sound a note in the second register her neck and throat become extremely tense and the larynx moves high in the throat. The consequent pull on the larynx exerted by the weight of the trachea destroys the possibility of good muscular use at laryngeal level. The first thing to put right is the overall body use, as discussed earlier. Then the breathing must be supported without collapse being allowed so that the pulling down is quite eliminated. When these conditions are functioning it is time to try to rescue the top of the voice – *but not before.*

The miaow

This is a gentle introduction to the work of opening up the top of the speaking range. It is, as you might suppose from the name of the exercise, to imitate the action of the cat – and miaow.

Think of the miaow starting very forward in the nose with the [m] and then open the lips to let the vowels out, thinking of the sound as travelling across the roof of the mouth from the soft palate forward towards the top teeth.

Inhibit the tendency of the throat to tighten. Instead of using throat tension to push at the sound, use the firm support of the breath instead.

Gradually allow the miaow more range until it starts in head and finishes fairly low in chest.

*But see Husler and Rodd-Marling, op. cit.

Don't try to make the sound loudly and, using the finger test, make sure you can't feel breath passing the lips.

Now it is time to move on to using the glide to extend the range. Remember that this is a slow business; it needs time for muscles to become used to new relationships and, probably, for some actual development of muscle.

The glide: stage 2
Once you can glide easily between second and first registers without the pitch-break, reverse the glide.

Starting on a comfortable low note in first register, move the note up through the middle of the voice into second register. The conditions for performing the upward glide are the same as for the downward glide – the neck, jaw and throat are free, and the breath well supported.

Now you are operating the glide from top to bottom and from bottom to top, allow yourself to work to your comfortable limits in both directions. Gradually you will find these limits are further apart. The voice will come to sound fuller and firmer carrying brightness and 'ring' throughout its now integrated range.

With the glide operating well in both directions it's time to use it for speech.

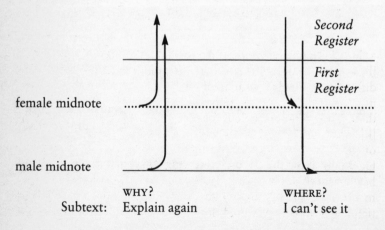

	WHY?	WHERE?
Subtext:	Explain again	I can't see it

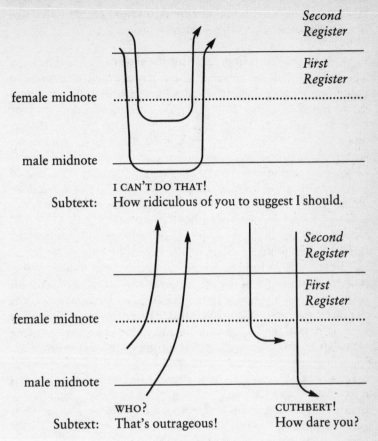

Subtext: How ridiculous of you to suggest I should.

Subtext: WHO? CUTHBERT!
That's outrageous! How dare you?

You may find with the introduction of unvoiced consonants [h, k, θ] that the pitch-break returns. This is not a matter for discouragement. Try to think of the *voice-shape* of the back of the mouth and throat staying active while you make the consonants so there is no sudden closing of the throat as you say them. Even with [k] (where the back of the tongue rises to meet the soft palate) think of the space *behind* the consonant barrier being wide open. The higher the note, too, the more you need to think of opening up the back of the mouth – until it has become the most comfortable way to work. At the least sign of discomfort in the throat, particularly tightening or aching, stop, release, and only go back to the work when you have had a good rest from it. Never push for the high notes – allow them to develop in ease and comfort.

High notes: the cover

The difficulty of using our very high notes with a fullness of resonant tone is one of the problems most often met with in voice production. As the note gets higher and higher, the opening and closing of the cords becomes faster and the size of the glottic opening gets shorter and narrower. There comes a point in our pitch-range when, if we were to go on producing the voice in the same way, the cords would be virtually jammed shut and to pass air between them would require so much force that the cords would be damaged and we would get a sore throat or voice strain. When we approach this point we have two ways of easing the situation: one is to go into falsetto and the other is to change the relationship between the larynx and the pharynx and in so doing change the use of the cords.

Towards the end of the nineteenth century, the Italian singing masters began to teach the use of something called 'the cover for open vowels' or 'the singer's passage'. The use of the Cover is a way of protecting the vocal cords during the singing of high notes; used with discretion, and as long as we are careful about the way we articulate the speech sounds, it can be of great service to the speaker. What happens during the use of the Cover is this: the larynx tips forward and down so that the relationship between the thyroid and cricoid cartilages changes and the vocal cords are lengthened. Because the cords are now longer, they are able to open wider while still maintaining the fast rate of opening and closing which the highest notes require. This change in the position of the larynx is accompanied by an enlargement of the pharynx which thereby continues to serve as a good resonator.

Without the use of the Cover, the highest notes are, as we have seen, forced, and what is more their resonance quality is meagre – they become what singers call 'white notes'. The thinness of sound is partly due to the fact that the larynx has been pulled high in the throat so that the overall size of the mouth/throat resonator is greatly diminished. Once the Cover is introduced, however, this all changes. An immediate easement of the over-tension in the throat takes place, the high notes which before seemed so difficult become much easier to manage, and a fullness of resonance comes back to the voice. The sensation which accompanies this act is rather like yawning, it is as if the whole back of the roof of the mouth has been lifted.

I said before that this technique needs to be used with discretion because if it is over-applied it can give the speaking voice a rather plummy quality which sounds pompous and quite far away from the quality of ordinary speech. But it isn't in 'ordinary' speech that you would be likely to want to use this technique. If you are playing a character of the kind that keeps screaming and having fits of hysterics you might find the Cover saves you from having to pull back the energy in your playing to a point where your hysterics are no longer believable, and it will certainly save you from having to be propped up by the laryngologist every time you give your performance the energy it calls for!

False limitations: the pressures of environment

The vocal range of an individual may be one thing as a physiological possibility and another thing in practice, as we've seen; and what makes people opt for limitations of voice use which they could quite easily escape is usually a combination of environmental pressures. We learn a great deal of our speaking voice use by imitation of those constantly around us. This can sometimes produce strange anomalies. I remember one actor who persistently tried to talk like a bass although it caused him a lot of strain and the result was quite horrible to hear. One day I met his father and elder brother, and it struck me that this actor was imitating *their* voice use – they both had rich and unforced bass-baritone voices. In discussion, the actor said it had never occurred to him that he was imitating the family voice, but certainly his ideal of what a man's voice should be was the sound his father and brother made – particularly the father, who had been a professional singer. Shortly after this conversation he began to use his voice in an easier way – easier for him and the audience.

Family models can exert a strong influence, not always for the good; so too can national or regional vocal fashions. These may be responsible for damaging patterns of voice use which owe nothing to the intrinsic quality of the language itself – such as Australian nasalization, for example, which can get in the way of the development of the lower voice. In Chile, Spanish is spoken with wide-ranging inflexional melodies and the higher and lighter qualities in the voice are dominant. In Spain there seems to be a general preference for low voices, especially for men, and the acting profession is to some extent bedevilled by it and by what seems to be a nationwide preoccupation with the low notes. (This is sometimes taken to absurd lengths; in the film-dubbing industry, for example, where mellifluous bass and baritone voices are made to come from bodies which simply could not have produced them.) A result of this preoccupation is that those actors who do not naturally have deep voices, and who perhaps have little or bad vocal training, are led to force their voices down to unnatural depths of note until a rasping false bass quality is heard. Often this produces such a strain on the vocal cords that they become permanently inflamed and develop nodules. It is not uncommon to meet Spanish actors who by early middle age have no range left to their voices and who can't lift the note unless they work on a shout. The strain in such cases is enormous. Producing the voice in this way is wasteful of energy and the actor finds himself physically quite exhausted at the end of his performance.

A lot of this strain comes about because the actor is confused about the difference between resonance and pitch. There is a common fallacy which supposes that low notes must be richly resonant; in fact they are only richly resonant if the voice is well resonated, and actors who push to stay on their very lowest notes often cheat themselves of the full richness of resonance available to them; the *note* may be low, but the quality is breathy or thin or muffled and sometimes it sounds as though the voice is produced between sheets of sandpaper. There is a limit to the height and depth of note available to any one voice and that has to be accepted as a physical fact. Also, in general, the lowest two or three tones we are capable of phonating are not much use for anything except microphone work because the vocal cords function in such a way that it is impossible to produce a lot of volume on these tones without strain. However, if the resonators are sensibly exploited, even quite high notes can sound rich and full – giving the impression that they belong to a low voice because they are enriched with a great deal of harmonic reverberation. This is a better approach than forcing things; it increases the range of the voice and takes the strain off the throat.

One more thing; most actors can in fact increase their vocal range because they don't normally use the *full* range which would be available if they consistently worked the voice sensibly. In this way it is possible that some actors who fondly imagine that they are using their lowest notes are in fact doing no such thing because they are forcing their whole vocal apparatus into malfunction.

Trying to fill the space

When we talk to an audience, we are trying to reach them. We make contact with the voice, but often it is as if we want to cross the distance between us physically as well, and this can lead to problems: specifically, the head wants to go in the direction we are talking, and if it does, we disturb the head/neck relationship and squash the neck and throat; also, in trying to reach a specific point, we can easily start to push the voice, raise the pitch too high and start talking *at* the audience rather than to them or with them. In this case, paradoxically, our very desire to reach the audience can make a barrier between us. There is a way round this problem which leaves our intention to communicate with the audience functioning properly as the directing force behind what we are doing, and which easily and naturally encourages the voice to operate fully at whatever volume is necessary but without our apparently having to 'speak up' or strain to be heard.

Exercises for filling the space

We began the business of producing the whole voice by getting the whole body to buzz with the sound – we filled ourselves with voice. Now, instead of trying to *reach* toward the audience, we are going to fill the space around us – all around us – thinking of ourselves as being the radiating centre of that space and, although we know the voice is coming out of our mouth, thinking that it is coming from every part of us, particularly from the back. We have to fill the space behind us and above us, to the sides as well as in front. In other words, it is the Body Buzz extended in all directions. This is an image, but not far from a just description of what actually happens. As an image, or direction if you like, it will help us not to throw out the head/neck relationship and sensitize us to more of our immediate environment than might otherwise be the case. We are the centre of our voice.

Another trick which can help is to think of the voice coming back to you from the furthest parts of the space you are working in. This is an old music-hall technique, and again the point of it is to avoid strain in the throat by not trying to push the voice out.

One more way of thinking of filling the space is to suppose that it is merely an extension of yourself – not something 'out there' separate from you which you have to push into. You are the space, the audience is part of you, and you keep filling yourself with the sound, a self as large as the space. Resonance happens in partially enclosed spaces; the larger the space, the richer the resonance. The outer space, being a continuation of the inner space, forms one huge resonator with it.

All these methods of filling the space depend on your intention. If you are talking directly to an audience there is no problem since part of your action in the scene is to make the audience hear. But what if you are playing an intimate scene on stage? Won't the fact that you are talking with someone other than the audience affect the voice use? Won't the intimacy of the scene mean you have to change the voice quality? Surely the voice can no longer be used as for a public address! No of course it can't, and yes the quality will change, following the motivation you give yourself as the character in the situation; but always you are the actor, and you are acting with other actors and for the audience as well as for yourself and the others who are on stage with you. So part of *your* motivation, whatever the motivation you may have ascribed to your character, and however intimate the scene, is to include the audience; it is always to fill your space: the theatre is your space, think of the theatre as you.

All this is an act of the imagination which has a direct effect upon the vocal mechanism. The process described is not scientifically approached, although the effects are exactly measurable in frequencies, harmonics, decibels and the like. Because the approach here is not scientific but suggestive, depending a great deal on the workings of the imagination, it might seem as though we are straying from the path of technical exercise and accomplishment into a woolly state of make-believe. But at some point, with the voice as with movement, as with the whole process of acting, or that of gripping the audience with a speech, we must wed imagination and science to make a technique which can fitly serve us in the artistry we propose. Now is that point.

Changing the resonance

So far you have worked to establish what we might call the normally produced, fully resonated, free sound – the voice which your body most easily produces when you don't get in the way. Now you must find out what else the voice can do; because until you discover your resources you are unlikely to use them. You have to some extent worked changes in the resonance of your voice in opening up the mouth/throat resonator, and you have worked to improve the quality of the nasal resonance as well. These are the basics in resonance. But every change in the position of the organs of articulation brings about a change of resonance, and if you include the changes which occur as a result of movements of the larynx in relation to the pharynx, and of the pharynx itself as it expands and contracts in the many ways it can, then you may come to realize that you possess a phenomenally wide range of resonance possibilities – wider by far than you ever explore. Not all of these possibilities of course will be useful for ordinary speech, but there is no limit to the demands the theatre may make upon the actor's resources. So here follow some suggestions for playing with the voice to *find out* what it can do.

Exercises for resonance

The three-tone

This is a simple exercise just to get you going. Keep to the *same note* throughout the changes which follow.

1 Sing [ɑː], directing the voice as usual on to the front of the hard palate.

2 Without either making a nasal consonant or losing the *vowel* quality of the sound, direct the voice-stream into the nose so that the vowel is nasalized.

3 Now direct the sound away from the nose and to resonate as

fully as possible in the pharynx; you have lifted the soft palate, and it is as if the note is pushing up the back of the roof of the mouth.

4 Now do the circuit again, and when you come back to resonate the mouth, think of the resonance moving right forward on to the teeth; the sound will thin out becoming bright and hard and as if there is almost no throat resonance; you will probably also observe that the larynx has moved up high. When you take the sound into the nose the front of the mouth will feel inert, but the nose and the back part of the hard palate will vibrate, and the larynx may move down a little. As you go for the pharyngeal resonance with the soft palate lifted, you will find that the larynx is comparatively low in the throat. While you are changing the quality of sound, be careful not to over-tighten the tongue – you don't want to get a sore throat.

End the exercise by balancing the resonance and directing the voice into and from the front of the hard palate.

Directing the sound

What you have been doing is directing the placing of the sound, making quite large movements of the soft palate, larynx and so on. But there are many possible small adjustments of these organs which can produce the more subtle changes in the voice. A difference in the amount of tonus in the various muscles, without great movements taking place, will produce a change in the resonance; a change in the air-pressure or in the amount of the airstream being turned into voice will make a difference in the sound. The possibilities are endless, and because some of these changes in the speech organs are very small, it is not much use trying to work for them by focusing your attention directly on those organs. But in order to provoke those changes in the speech organs you can play with your mental *direction* of the voice, and you will notice that the voice changes in consequence as you do.

What happens, for example, when you direct the voice to sound from the breast bone just below the point where it joins with the collar bones? What happens when you change that direction and think of the voice coming from your back? Or as if you are bringing the sound down from the frontal sinuses and out through the nostrils, but without making the voice nasal in tone? It's up to you how far you are willing to take your experimentation, but the more of it you do, the more you will know what you *can* do. And if you want a change from directing the voice into and from various parts of your body, try directing the voice as if it is coming from various points outside the body: from the ceiling, the floor and so on. Some of these directives may produce no notable change; this doesn't matter; others will surprise you with qualities of sound you will not have imagined beforehand.

The band

Imitation is a great help in finding out what you can do. Try, for example, singing a song mostly on vowels and orchestrating it: give each phrase to a different instrument – saxophone, shawm, tuba – whatever takes your fancy. Then try turning the various noises into speech and see what they suggest by way of characterization; after all, however strange the sound you are producing, it *is* human sound and you can probably make a safe bet that someone, somewhere, is producing his voice in that way in ordinary life!

The zoo

When you've tried being a band, try to find the zoo which lives in you. Imitate animal noises. You can take this much further than noise-making, and develop it into a good acting exercise as you study animal behaviour and find its human translation. We shall have more to do with this later on in the voice and movement work. But starting with the sound at this point is useful because it gets you away from the noises you usually make – just as The Band does – and by moving away from self-as-known you find some of the many selves-unknown.

Other people

Finally I suggest that you study other people. Analyse how they produce their basic voice sound and see if you can produce it as well. This is the richest study of all in the imitative process. How do others change their voice quality in response to shifts of mood and intention? Does the nature of a person's work influence the quality of sound he makes? What effect does age, social condition, health have on the voice? In this, try, as part of the analytic process to see beyond accent and eccentricities of speech and vocabulary to the matrix of the voice itself. The study of speech patterns, and of body use, and the rhythm at which somebody lives are all important to us in our observation, but for the moment, listen to and then try to reproduce the voice.

Volume control

If you are taking care to tune the voice efficiently for note and resonance, the volume control should work for most of your range. But low notes are difficult to sound loudly; and there is always the tendency for high notes to be sounded with too much volume, although the foregoing exercises should have helped in this regard. Since it is the relationship between breath pressure and the vocal cords which governs the volume, we must turn our attention to breath control as part of the business of achieving control of the volume.

Exercises for volume control

Sound a note, hold it steady, keep the placing or direction of the voice-stream constant and gradually increase the volume.

Make sure that as the pressure exerted by the abdominal muscles increases, the breath doesn't rush out of you: in other words, don't let the voice get breathy. When you release the out-breath muscles and allow the breath in again, permit the full expansion of the rib-cage, particularly in the back and to the sides.

If you refuse to let the note go breathy and the rib-cage to collapse or pull down, you will find that the following happens, supposing the note is sounded quite loudly: at the moment you sound the note the abdominal muscles contract to pressurize the breath supply; because of the upward displacement of the viscera and the downward pressure of the diaphragm upon the viscera, and because the cords are letting comparatively little air through, there is an all-round lateral displacement of the rib-cage, most noticeable at the level of the lower ribs and this includes the muscle between the costal arch just below the breast bone; also, the breast bone itself tends to rise slightly. As the note continues,

gradually this expansion is lost and the whole rib-cage decreases
its girth. There is no loss of length as you breathe out.

Now you need to practise gradually increasing the volume on your
lower notes, always holding whichever note you are working on
in tune; don't allow variation of breath pressure to influence your
pitching of the note. Also, continue the note to the end of your
manageable breath without allowing the volume to fade. It may
help to think that you are actually getting longer and wider while
you do this – you won't, but thinking in this way will help you
not to collapse. With practice the note will be louder and longer.

Now you can practise this control up the scale until you have gone
through that part of your range where you find the control
relatively easy; as you hit the top notes you will want to increase
the volume to sustain the pitch, so at this moment you begin to
practise keeping the volume down. Be careful about the direction
of the voice-stream and don't lose the sense of focusing it at the
forward part of the hard palate. Keep the tongue as free as you
can.

When you get to the high notes which begin to make you feel as
though you are near your limit and to go higher would be to force
the voice, employ the Cover (see The Pitch-Break: Registers). Go
gently here. You will find it easier to control the volume, but you
will probably find some difficulty in maintaining the direction
and placing. It is a question of practice, and of inhibiting any
tendency to tighten the tongue and the neck.

Using the phrases 'How are you?' and 'Hey! You over there!' give
yourself a series of different motivations which call for gradually
increasing volume. As the volume goes up be careful you don't
allow the breath support to collapse, the neck to tighten or the
head to poke forward. You must also guard against airspill – use
the finger test. As the volume gets near to a shout or cry, you will
feel the action of the abdominal muscles as a firm inward pull
toward the spine – much as in the exercise Blowing Out Candles.
(You will also notice the breast bone has a tendency to lift, the
muscle in the costal arch to push forward and the lower ribs to
push out sideways. Don't try to make these things occur – allow
them: they are the natural consequences of the diaphragm

beginning to assert its own specific tendency to flatten downward.)

Volume control is not something which just happens because you know how to do it. It requires a great deal of practice to accustom the muscles to working in new ways. Ten minutes of careful attention to it should hereafter be part of your daily workout.

Shouting

The volume control which you have been practising, together with the breathing exercise Blowing Out Candles (p. 57), provides the basis from which you can shout without fear of hurting the throat. But shouting, as distinct from merely talking loudly, usually has a large emotional drive – pain, fear, anger, surprise, joy – and the emotion can take over and produce misplaced tensions which can be damaging, especially the more 'down' emotions. So when you are practising, it's a good idea to work your way gently, being careful about the motivation you use, and keeping a monitoring eye and ear open.

Exercises for shouting
The following sequence may serve as a guide:

1 Begin by producing the voice loudly and fully but not yet at a shouting level. Check the tuning and don't blow out a lot of unresonated air. Use a vowel sequence, but imagine a communicative purpose.

2 Begin to remotivate the sequence. Give yourself the necessary background situation – say, the sudden reappearance of a long-lost friend. Let the vowel sequence be the joyful and surprised greeting. Go through the small scene a few times, letting the joy and the surprise grow with each version until it has become a rapture of celebration. Out of the need to express the joyful surprise comes the voice: let the voice be the *product* of the emotional communicative impulse.

3 As the impulse gets bigger, and the voice gets bigger with it, keep

your monitor working; check on your use and the noise you are making; inhibit that first tendency to turn yourself into a tight knot of tension in the neck and tongue; keep the voice well supported, which has a freeing effect on the expression of the emotion. Then take the vowel sequence into words, but keep the phrases short to begin with. If the words pose difficulties and you find some sounds are tugging at the throat, you will probably find an explanation as to why, and what to do about it, in the next section of the book.

Tuning the voice to a particular range

Most of the information about how to do this has been covered previously in this section, but there remains one important point to be made. If your part demands that you use a small part of your range and a part which you do not find easy to pitch with consistency, you will find difficulty in establishing the keynote, that note to which the voice returns again and again in normal speech and which indicates a point of arrival, usually at the end of a statement. Suppose the chosen range is going to be very high, you may find as you make the ordinary statement that the voice slides down towards your normal keynote; the result is a swooping series of inflexions which sound quite unreal. Or you may find that your awareness that you *want* to swoop down to your normal keynote stops you from arriving at *anything* which can be called a keynote, so the voice sounds drifting and without the definition which would normally be there. The answer to both of these problems is the same and lies in the way you motivate what you are doing. If you approach the change of pitch as a mechanic and allow your technical preoccupations to oust your actor's intention the problem will remain. If you keep the intention of the action and play that, *together* with your use of pitch change, you will find the problem disappears.

SPEECH

Introduction

There are two kinds of activity which we perform when we speak. The first is linguistic and is the choosing of the noises, words and phrases which will convey our communicative intention. The second is mechanical, the articulation of the basic units of speech sound so that they become words and phrases and are made audible to the audience.

Here we begin with the mechanical principles of speech, relating the forming of speech sounds to the use of the breath and to the tuning of the voice, and also, most importantly, to the good use of self which supports all of our voice work.

So this section of the book is about how speech sounds may help or hinder good voice use. It isn't a detailed guide to the pronunciation of Standard English. The principles which govern the work and the exercises apply equally to all forms of English pronunciation.

However, since the speech exercises assume the use of Standard English and such phonetic symbols as are used refer to Standard English models, a brief word about this particular form of pronunciation is needed by way of explanation.

Standard English or Received Pronunciation

Standard English is generally held to be the least regional of the English accents. It's based on Southern speech, however, and is influenced by such factors as the pronunciation prevalent in public schools and universities, television and radio. Its sources are so widespread that a precise definition of it is impossible here. Furthermore it is constantly changing and the standard pronunciation of a

word for one generation may be old-fashioned and rarely used by
the next. A good general guide to the pronunciation of individual
words is the *Everyman English Pronouncing Dictionary* by Daniel
Jones; this is brought up to date every few years.

Actors are generally required to learn Standard English and it
does provide a useful basis for any study of English pronunciations,
simply because it is less coloured by specific regional and class
usages than other forms of English pronunciation. But it is not
necessarily the best English accent for producing maximum resonance in the voice. Some Scots, Welsh and Northern English accents
open the resonators much more effectively and lead to a better voice
placement in the natural way of things. However, Standard English
is a clear form of pronunciation, easily understood by most people
who speak English, and it's certainly not the worst accent for
resonance purposes.

The accent itself, like any accent, is difficult to describe in the
written form even with the aid of phonetics* and is best learned by
direct tuition and with the use of a tape recorder. (See Working on
Accents, pp. 189–92.)

The speech organs

Most of the speech organs are in the mouth: the lips, the teeth, the
tongue and the palate. The vocal cords may also be considered as
speech organs, and in some languages the false vocal cords may
have a function in articulating speech sounds.

The tongue is the most flexible of the speech organs and can be
moved in several different ways at the same time. For the sake of
convenience in describing the formation of sounds we distinguish
the parts of the tongue as follows (this description presupposes the
tongue is lying relaxed in the floor of the mouth with the tip resting
against the bottom front teeth): the *tip* is the extreme front edge of

---

*Where necessary I have noted distinctions between the customary phonetic
transcription of American English and Standard English. I have also noted some
principal differences in the formation of sounds. However, the purpose here is not
so much to explore differences of pronunciation as to see how the *voice* may be
freed in speech. The exercises help to do that whether given a Standard English or
American English pronunciation.

the tongue; the *blade* that part immediately behind the tip which lies under the alveolar ridge. In the body of the tongue the *front* lies under the hard palate, the *back* under the soft palate and the area where front and back meet is known as the *centre*. The *sides* of the tongue (sometimes called the *rims*) have great mobility and are responsible for shaping some consonants. The *root* does not directly make speech shapes at all but has a large part to play in determining the resonance quality of the voice; it is the extreme back curve of the tongue and the part which anchors the tongue in the jaw. The tip and blade together shape some of the consonants; the front, centre and back of the tongue shape the vowels and some consonants.

The palate, too, may be considered according to the function of its various parts. The *hard palate* reaches back from the top teeth; there is a bony ridge where the teeth socket into the palate and this is called the *alveolar ridge*. Extending back across the roof of the mouth from the end of the hard palate is the *soft palate* which ends in the *uvula*. Each part of the palate helps to shape various consonants, and in addition, the soft palate, which is muscular, governs the air-flow from the throat to the nose.

The speech act

When the tuned voice-stream passes through the mouth during speech, a complicated series of rapid movements performed by the speech organs changes its quality from speech sound to speech sound. In general these changes are of two kinds: those which merely reshape the resonator, changing thereby the resonance of the voice, but offering no effective barrier to the airstream – these are the *vowels*; and those which do form barriers, partial or complete as the case may be, and these are the *consonants*.

The voice-stream is mainly carried on the vowels. The consonants, which, as it were, chop up the voice-stream, help give definition and shape to it by imposing separations between vowels. Further shape is given to the voice/breath-stream as we make *syllables*, which are the rhythm and energy units of speech.

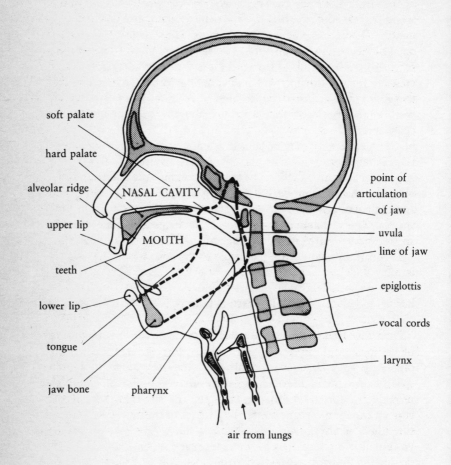

soft palate

hard palate

alveolar ridge

NASAL CAVITY

upper lip

MOUTH

teeth

lower lip

tongue

jaw bone

pharynx

point of
articulation
of jaw

uvula

line of jaw

epiglottis

vocal cords

larynx

air from lungs

25 The speech organs

Syllables

Speech is an energetic process, and the clarity of our speech depends upon how well we use our energy. The syllable is the basic unit of speech energy. It may consist of one speech sound or of a combination of speech sounds. For example the single sound 'ah', [ɑ:], is one syllable, and so is the word 'grinds', [graɪndz], which contains seven different sounds. There are many possible variations. The constant factor is that each syllable, no matter how many sounds there are in it, has its own pulse of energy. Later, to help our speech work we shall make an artificial division of the syllable into its constituent vowels and consonants and consider them separately, but for all practical purposes, in real connected speech the syllable is the smallest unit.

What makes a syllable is the combination of two things: *the muscular changes in the organs of articulation* which form the speech-shapes, and the *impulse of breath* which passes through the speech-shapes and which may be voiced or not according to the speech sounds being made.

Each energetic impulse is primarily powered by the breath which is put under pressure by a contraction of the rib-cage and the abdominal muscles. Usually these contractions are so slight that we hardly feel them. In ordinary connected speech we make these contractions, one for each syllable, at the rate of about five a second.

Each time that we make a syllable there is a build-up and release of air-pressure in the vocal tract, and of tension in the appropriate organs of articulation, so one of the characteristics of ordinary speech is that the voice comes and goes unevenly as the syllables are made. This uneven quality in our speech is what provides it with rhythm and if it were missing we should find it difficult to distinguish the shapes of the words. And yet we are to develop a use of the voice which is based on a *continuous flow* of resonance. Why we do this and how the apparent contradiction it involves is reconciled is described in the section Maximum Definition and Minimum Effort. First we'll consider the special demands that the auditorium imposes on the speaker.

Sung speech and conversation

Let's consider what happens in opera and conversation; speech is used in both these forms of communication but in very different ways.

The singer's art is to make speech sounds musical. To do this the singer tunes and sustains speech sounds and the sustaining is usually done with the vowels. The singer has to produce a tone which will carry to the audience over the background noise of the orchestra. So that the overall size of the throat/mouth resonator may be kept large and the outgoing musical tone meet as small an obstruction as possible, the interior of the mouth is closed as little as possible during the formation of the consonants. The more singers can rest on the vowels the happier they are. This may lead to certain distortions of pronunciation, but since generally the singer's main communication is through the music and not verbal, these distortions are practical given the singer's overall objectives.

With normal conversational speech we are at the opposite end of things. Most conversation takes place across a relatively small space and without a lot of background noise. In conversation we have no need for an artificially contrived voice production; as long as it's audible and conveys our intention, any quality of resonance will do. We have no particular need for great definition of the speech sounds as long as the person we are talking to has an equal fluency in the language; we can use incomplete words, words elided together, broken phrases, and these will serve very well, particularly if the other person can see our lips and read our expressions and our gestures. The need for breath conservation doesn't arise; we can shape our thoughts into phrases which accommodate our breathing.

Speech in the theatre

But if you talk in such a way on the stage of a large theatre, that part of the audience which is not very close to the stage will find it difficult to understand what's being said. They'll hear speech noises going on but so lacking in definition that they have to strain to catch the words: it's the acoustic equivalent of looking through the wrong end of a slightly unfocused telescope; the distance between speaker and audience is emphasized and the speaker seems diminished in consequence because such sound lacks a theatre-filling quality. The audience needs more than merely to hear the words; it wants to feel comfortable with the business of hearing, and to be able to catch the least nuance without strain. For this your voice must be full enough to sound as though it belongs in that space.

How to keep the *voice* full and well resonated so that it comfortably fills the space of a theatre has been examined in detail (see Tuning). But the use of connected speech (rather than a series of more or less extended vowels) can bring problems when the voice is used with full resonance and more loudly than in ordinary room-sized conversation.

Usually actors want to sound as though they are speaking as normally in the theatre as they might in a small room. If you are playing a naturalistic part, most of the interruptions, elisions and irregularities of normal speech will need to be reproduced; and even if you're playing a highly wrought text which departs from normal speech rhythms to some extent, say a piece of Shakespeare which uses metre and rhyme, you still don't want your speech sounds to seem distorted. If in real life you say the phrase 'give me a ten pound note' as 'gimme a tempoun ote', ['gɪmiə 'tempaʊn ‿əʊt], you don't want to make it seem like a diction exercise on stage and enunciate every possible sound with exaggerated clarity, ['gɪv 'mi: eɪ 'ten ˌpaʊnd 'nəʊt]. You may, if you find your ordinary diction confusing to the audience, modify it a little while still keeping the ordinary speech rhythm, and perhaps the phrase might end up as ['gɪv miə 'tempaʊn ‿'nəʊt], 'give me a tempoun ‿note'. This would be acceptable ordinary sounding speech.

The Problems

1 Ordinary speech, even at its slowest, is still a series of very fast movements of the speech organs. It's comfortable when you're speaking fast to leave the jaws as close together as you can. But when you want to produce a full resonance as well, if you keep the jaws closed you rob yourself of resonating space in the mouth and perhaps drive the voice into the nose. On the other hand, you don't want your jaw snapping open and shut in an exaggerated way – you want to look normal as well as sound it.

2 As you speak more loudly the thoracic/abdominal contractions
   tend to become more violent because of the need for an increase
   of pressure in the breath supply; where the voice is properly tuned
   this increase of pressure is a help in maintaining increased volume,
   but even so it can put undue emphasis on those parts of speech
   where there is no voice – the unvoiced consonants, which may
   become puffy; this in turn may lead to the whole speech pattern
   becoming too breathy.

3 Also, during loud speech, the organs of articulation tend to move
   more strongly in making and releasing the consonantal barrier.
   If they move too strongly this can have three effects:
   a) The over-tensed speech organs become less responsive; quick,
      light articulation becomes difficult and the consonants become
      overemphatic and clumsy.
   b) The second effect is that the release of the over-tensed
      consonant-shape, and with it the breath-stream, may provoke
      a rush of untuned air so that, again, the speech becomes
      breathy.
   c) The third effect may be that as the organs of articulation work
      harder and harder, the supportive action of the breath-stream,
      the carrier of the voice, is reduced to a point where the speech
      seems to be all consonant and the voice remains bottled-up.
      This last effect is serious, because the tension created by the
      organs of articulation tends to be communicated to the whole
      breathing system which may then go into reverse (see
      Breathing) and fail to support the voice. When this happens,
      usually the speaker makes too much effort to push the voice
      out from the throat which becomes very tense in consequence
      and the cords suffer strain.
   All of these inefficient uses of speech come from misapplying the
   energy and making *too much work* for the speech organs;
   remedies follow in the next section.

4 But there are cases, of course, when the speech is unclear because
   the organs of articulation are not doing enough work and the
   voice-stream is allowed to smother the consonants. In the worst
   of such cases, the speech seems to be all vowels and no consonant.
   The cure for this lies in training the speech organs to make the
   speech-shapes clearly and firmly; and often this can be done most

effectively by using a whisper but allowing as little of the breath as possible to support the articulatory movements. This *makes* the speech muscles function. Aim to hear every sound distinctly while you do this, but do not lose the normal rhythmic flow of the speech. When you can, without losing this clarity produced by the exact and efficient use of the speech organs, bring the voice back into use. The voice/breath-stream should still be well tuned and a dramatic overall improvement in the clarity of speech should be evident.

In adapting our speech for the stage we find ourselves with a use which is somewhere between that of ordinary conversation and singing. The vowels are made to carry most of the vocal tone but a clear, undistorted articulation of consonants is used as well.

Assessing your speech clarity

Sometimes it's quite difficult to know whether or not one's speech is unclear. Most people, after all, find little difficulty in making their words understood in everyday conversation. If you are thrown back on your own resources and don't have the help of a trained observer or teacher, try to get hold of a good tape recorder, with a detachable microphone; self-adjusting microphones of the sort that are often built in to recorders should be avoided because they falsify the evidence too much. Make a few recordings of yourself giving an address, reading a story or a poem or using a speech from a play. Imagine yourself in the performing situation, put the microphone where you imagine the audience to be, and let rip. The recording will help you arrive at an objective idea of what your voice and speech sound like. When you've listened to the recording and made your own deductions play it to a friend and see if everything comes across clearly. The friend won't have the benefit of knowing the text, as you do, nor of seeing you speak – an audience is greatly helped in understanding your words by watching the movements of your lips – so this is quite a stern test of the clarity of your speech.

The tape recorder is a great help in the tricky business of assessing the clarity of your speech and I would advise the frequent use of it when you are doing the speech exercises which follow. Not all tape recorders, however, are faithful speech reproducers. Often they will distort the basic resonance of the voice and the sound of the sibilant consonants. Test your recorder by recording someone else and at different distances from the microphone/s. If the reproduction sounds accurate, well and good – otherwise keep searching. A poor recorder is worse than useless.

Maximum definition and minimum effort

Physical predispositions

If speech is formed at the rate of approximately five syllables a second, how on earth can you think about forming each sound as it comes along? You don't; what you do is make sure your basic predispositions for speech are right and cultivate enough speech agility to be able to form the sounds properly, so that as you speak, you easily and naturally take advantage of your right predispositions. The physical predispositions for clear speech are as follows:

Keep the joint of the jaw open and free at all times and don't worry how far apart the teeth are – allow the jaw to move freely as it needs.

Think of the breath-stream as being, as far as possible, a continuing flow of tuned voice.

Keep the muscular activity in shaping the consonants as light and precise as possible.

These three points are the direct follow-through into speech of the Good Use you began to practise with the first exercises. Keeping the jaw free and a light, precise use of the speech organs is only an extension of keeping the neck free. You are aiming for maximum definition in your speech with minimum effort.

An experiment

Say the syllable 'pee', [pi:], at first normally and then with increasing volume and see what happens.

Observe the facial muscles as the sound gets louder, and listen for any change in the resonance.

Probably you will find that the cheeks and lips get tenser. You may also notice that the consonant becomes more marked and the vowel more breathy. If neither of these things happens and you keep a full resonation of the vowel, that's good.

If, however, they do happen, stop your first response (to tighten the muscles of face, mouth and throat), then, keeping the neck free and the action of the lips and cheeks to the minimum required for the clear articulation of the consonant, concentrate on the quality of resonance in the vowel.

It may help to shape the vowel in the mouth by way of preparation, then, retaining the vowel shape, to shape the consonant. So in effect the lips are closed for [p] in front of the prepared [i:]. Then the full syllable in pronounced.

After a bit of trial and error you will find it is quite possible to say the syllable loudly with an adequate articulation of the [p] and with the [i:] fully resonant. You may also notice that the less work you allow the face, mouth and throat to do, the more you work from lower down; or, conversely, you will find the jaw and tongue free up as your supported voice does more of the work.

As the air is more efficiently tuned, the pressure on the lips is lessened and in consequence they can release into a light barrier which is just sufficient to stop the breath-stream and form the [p] which is easily released to let the voice out on [i:].

At this point, test the economy of your breath use. Put a finger just before the lips as you say [pi:]. You should feel very little air as you say [p] and none as you say [i:].

Now make a two syllable sound: 'pee-pah', [pi: pɑ:] and think again of keeping the inside of the mouth prepared to make the vowels and make the consonants as lightly as possible. If most or too much of the energy is in the consonant you will feel the work going on in your mouth, throat and face, but if the energy is mainly in the tuned voice-stream you will feel a connection exists between your whole body and your voice; the sounds will be clear and the feeling of tension in the speech organs will be diminished. Of course it is possible to overdo the release of the lips and end up with a fluffy [p] which lacks definition and a true plosive quality; this is a question of judgement.

What works for 'Pee' and 'Pah' will also be found to work for any combination of vowel and consonant. Try repeating the experiment with different combinations of your own choice.

The vowel-chain

As we join syllables together into words and phrases, the syllabic thrust is determined by the importance of the syllable in the rhythmic structure of the word and the sense value of the word in the phrase, and is indicated by changes of pitch and volume and length of sound. Wherever the stresses fall, and however great the changes of pitch and volume, they should make no difference to the fundamental method of shaping the speech sounds. But if a stressed syllable begins with a consonant, and particularly if the consonant is either plosive or unvoiced, there is a tendency to distort the speech in some of the ways mentioned above (see Speech in the Theatre: The Problems). Part of the suggested remedial action was to prepare the vowel-shape in the mouth even during the making of the consonant. An enlargement and follow-through of this may be practised with the Vowel-Chain exercise.

The vowel-chain exercise

1 Take a short phrase and say it vigorously until you're used to the sound, feel the rhythm of it:

Get out of here, Charlie!
[ˌget ˈaʊt əv ˌhɪə ˈtʃɑː lɪ]

Put a finger lightly on your lips as you say this, so you can feel the variations in the air-flow; perhaps something like this:

[ˌget ˈaʊt əv ˌhɪə ˈtʃɑː lɪ]

The more the underlining, the more the breath is felt on the finger.

2 Gradually drop the consonants until you're left with a chain of vowels, each joined to the next without a break but pronounced with the rhythm (i.e. the syllabic pulse) of the complete words:

[ˌe ‿ˈaʊ ‿ə ‿ˌɪə ‿ˈɑːɪ]

3 Now make sure the vowel-stream is well tuned. You should feel hardly anything but a gentle warmth on your finger. When the resonance is full and rich the mouth/throat resonator is properly open and you will be using the voice in a properly supported way.

4 Now gradually let the consonants come back into the phrase, but with the minimum action possible for light clear articulation, and keep the full resonation of the voice. Think of the vowels as flowing one into the other almost as if you were not making the consonants at all. Still your finger should merely feel a gentle warmth – no blowing and puffing. In this way the resonating space is kept open, particularly at the back of the mouth, and most of the work is being performed by the supported voice-stream.

You should end up with a clearly pronounced phrase which is not only as resonant as it can be but completely without distortion, even though you may chose to say it very loudly.

When this exercise is performed fluently you will notice the following: the back of the mouth feels very open, almost cave-like; the jaw feels loose; the facial muscles seem to be doing less work.

This is a simple way of relating the process of support to articulation of speech and may be profitably applied to the work paragraphs for consonants on pp. 147–67. But it is not, of course, anything more than a basic pattern of speech use. It's a neutral state. When you come to act you will want to make changes according to character and situation. Once you know what supported speech is you can make such changes as may be necessary and without sacrificing your clarity and control. With the foundations of good speech use laid, the rest is a question of common sense, trial and error and experience. If you hurt yourself and begin to feel uncomfortable in the throat then you are doing something wrong. You probably won't be able to go on doing it all through rehearsal and performance without losing your voice. At the first sign of vocal discomfort check:

1 the freedom of the head/neck/back relationship

2 the breath support

3 the freedom of the jaw

4 the tuning of the voice.

Voice energy and speech energy

What The Vowel-Chain seeks to do is encourage the connection between the speech act and the voice. Necessarily, unless you are whispering, you are using voice when you speak, but the difference between speech which has an effective voice connection and that which hasn't is enormous. It is as if two different kinds of energy are involved. We may, for convenience, describe these as 'voice energy' and 'speech energy'.

Speech energy makes for a sound which seems to originate somewhere in the mouth; it doesn't convey the impression that the whole of the speaker is involved; it sounds 'intellectual', 'gutless', 'sexless', 'uncentred', 'disconnected' . . . The opprobrious epithets are numerous and they are trying to describe a series of physical happenings, the chief of which is that the voice is not supporting the speech act. There *is* a disconnection – the voice is out of touch with the emotions.

Voice energy produces a sound which seems to involve the whole body and to be in direct touch with the source of the emotions. It occurs when the voice is properly supported. It transforms the affective quality of speech which becomes thereby a fit means of communicating not just our ideas but our whole emotional engagement – with the idea, ourselves, the person we're talking to and the complete situation of the moment. It puts the person in the word, and invites an empathetic response from the audience.

It seems we evolved to make loud emotion-driven vocal noise before we developed the faculty of speech. Certainly as babies we have from birth the ability to communicate our urgent needs effectively and across considerable distances by yelling, crying, screaming and the like; and, as we've noted before (see Babies and Football Fans), we can keep making these loud emotional noises for a long time, when we are babies, without damage. However, gradually we lose this ability; partly through the development of overall patterns of misuse, but partly also because we need these noises less and less as our vocal communication becomes increasingly symbolic, intellectual and verbal. Because in general we no longer need the loud emotion-driven noise, the muscular use which produced and supported it falls into decay. After all, we need very little voice in ordinary conversation; the meaning we intend to convey comes across through the word rather more than through the voice quality. The result is a general thinning and quietening of the voice and the development of precise, highly complex movements of the speech organs, which we can perform with great rapidity and very little emotional involvement. Indeed, if we feel intense emotion while speaking, it often has a locking effect on the voice and we can find ourselves almost incapable of framing the words well even when we have a clear idea of what we want to say.

At such moments there is a struggle taking place in the body; we experience unusual tensions in the abdomen, the throat, the chest; our breathing becomes disorganized. It is almost as though we are trying to find our way back to the atavistic yelling and screaming of childhood. But now our bodies are unused to it, and besides, the social inhibitions against such forms of expression in adults are very strong in most highly evolved societies. The result of this struggle is a locking of voice and word.

This locking is often given a psychological explanation, and in some cases that explanation may be the true one. There is in consequence a certain amount of voice work which centres on removing or breaking down psychological inhibition in order to free the voice. Some of this work is of great value and has helped to produce good results. However, in a body which is ill-prepared to produce fully connected voice energy, or where the necessary muscles don't work well because through long misuse or lack of use they have decayed in their vocal function, the voice will remain locked.

Most of the vocal locking which occurs with actors and performers under the stress of high emotion originates, in my view, with the fear that if we 'let go' we will damage ourselves – specifically, that we will damage the vocal mechanism. It is not necessarily perceived as such. What makes me suppose it to be so is the often observed fact that when actors have properly established the connection between their voice energy and speech energy the majority of these blocks disappear.

This is a question of psychological freedom coming from perceived physical ability. The body, indeed the whole person, feels safer to 'let go' when it knows it possesses the means whereby it can express the strong emotion in sound and without damage. There's nothing so encouraging to the doing of something as the finding that you *can* do it.

If the vocal mechanism is well connected through all of its parts as a functioning whole, we are necessarily in touch with, and motivating the voice from, the same source which gives us our emotional being; the two are inextricably linked.

As far as the socially originated inhibitions are concerned, actors and performers are licensed by society to explore and communicate the strongest of emotions, and to make whatever noise is necessary in the process. So, on the stage, the social inhibitions which lock the voice have no place and generally don't appear – however much the actor or singer may be affected by them in private life.

Exercise: kneeling

This is designed to get the voice energy supporting the speech; it helps you attain the automatic, fast release of the muscles responsible for the in-breath; it helps with jaw release and with getting the back working as part of the voice support.

1 Kneel, sitting back on your heels with your back straight. Allow your weight to go forward from the hip joint (following your head direction) until you're resting lightly on your hands and slightly more on your knees. Your back should still be straight and it should prove easy to rock backward and forward keeping it straight. Your whole torso, from hips to neck, including the full width of the shoulders, forms a flat table. The head should neither be pulled up nor dropped down. The relationship between the head, the neck and the back, even though the weight is being supported differently, should be the same as when you're standing.

2 Let gravity take the weight of your jaw and the muscles of the face – as if your face is falling towards the floor. Using gravity in

this way you should find it easy to open and shut the jaw while keeping it released. This helps open the back of the mouth – particularly if you don't tense the tongue.

3 Make sure you're not holding the abdominal muscles; allow the full weight of the guts to drop but without losing the flat table of the back.

4 Breathe out vigorously, as though blowing the floor clean. As you puff the breath out you will feel a quick, firm movement of the abdominal muscles inward towards the spine as the guts are lifted and supported. Don't lose the table of the back as you exhale; this would mean that you have lost some length in the back. As soon as you've puffed the air out, allow the guts to drop again – but *don't* allow the back to slump when you do so. You will find that you have inhaled without any conscious effort to do so. This is really the Candle Blowing exercise performed on all fours. The next stage is to use this action for vocalization.

5 Make a short, loud sound on a vowel:
'Ah!' [ɑ:]
The sound should be solid, with no trace of breathiness and also with no trace of glottalization. You should feel the same kind of movement in the abdominal muscles as in 4, although this time in fact you don't expel much air (the abdominal contraction is compressing the air to the pressure necessary for the loudness of the sound). Another, odder sensation is that when you make the sound, because the jaw is so loose, it's as if the abdominal contraction itself causes the jaw to open – or as if the voice is pushing the jaw open to make a way out.

6 Imagine a phrase, and, as in The Vowel-Chain, pronounce only the vowels, joining them smoothly together:
Where *are* you going?
[εə‿'ɑ: ‿u: ‿əʊɪ]
Leave the face and jaw loose and connect with the breath as above. This time the strong contraction of the abdominal muscles will be on the first syllable only and the tonus thus achieved will remain in the muscles until you have finished speaking, when you release the abdominal muscles as before by letting the guts drop.

7 Say the same phrase, but with the consonants as well. Form the
   consonants correctly but with the minimum disturbance of the
   loose jaw and the minimum effort of the organs of articulation.

8 Extend the phrase on the one breath:
           Where are you going to in such a hurry?
   Keep extending the phrase, without losing your breath connection
   or your looseness of jaw or the lightness of the articulation.

           Where are you going to in such a hurry
           this fine Sunday morning
           when the bells are ringing
           the sun is shining
           and everything invites you to take your time
           and stay a short while for a sociable chat . . .
   until you are speaking a very long phrase or sentence comfortably
   on one breath.

   Gradually you will notice that you can keep the open, strong
connection between the supported voice and the light and just
sufficiently energized articulation of the speech without having to
compress the guts so violently on the first syllable. As the diaphragm
begins to assert its own specific tendency to flatten you will find
that the pressure of the abdominal muscles is fairly constant, with
only minor adjustments even on major stresses. You will feel that
your back seems to widen all the time (this is partly illusion; the
back certainly widens as you breathe in and widens some more as
the breath is compressed when you begin to speak, but it narrows
considerably towards the end of the out-breath). You will also
probably notice a feeling of pressure under the breast bone and into
the ribs at the sides; perhaps also you will feel a forward pressure
between the costal arch. Throughout, attention should be given to
the direction of the head leading the back into length, and to the
free state of the jaw – and to the sensation that it is the energized
voice which is carrying the speech sounds out of the mouth.
   Repeat the long phrase standing, walking, sitting – until the
fully supported voice/speech connection can be easily maintained
whatever you're doing.
   If you have articulation problems with some of the exercise
paragraphs which follow later, it's a good idea to try the difficult

passages in the above way. The action of gravity helps keep the jaw free and you will more easily feel any tendency to overwork the speech organs. Also, there is no better aid to clear, light articulation of speech than to allow it to be carried, as it were, on the supported voice.

Vowels

We have only six symbols in written English (a, e, i, o, u, y) to represent a large number of spoken vowels, and one of these (y) is used to represent a consonant as well; so, in this table of vowels, there is a word containing the vowel sound, the word written phonetically, and then the phonetic symbol for the vowel.

Dots [:] after a symbol indicate the sound is lengthened.*

['] before a syllable indicates the following syllable is stressed. ['peɪlɪŋ] for 'Paling'.

[ˌ] before a syllable in a group of syllables indicates the following syllable has a secondary stress. [ˌɪndɪˈkeɪʃn] for 'Indication).

The simple vowels

Each vowel has its own slightly variable tongue position; the tip of the tongue may rest behind the bottom front teeth in all vowel positions while the body of the tongue shapes the vowel.

In order to feel the difference between the various vowel-shapes it helps if the teeth are a constant distance apart – open enough for you to be able to put a knuckle between them. Reading down the left hand column, the words form a mnemonic sentence in which 'and' and 'of' are given their fully stressed pronunciation.

who	[hu:]	[u:]	Lips firmly rounded, back of tongue raised.
would	[wʊd]	[ʊ]	Lips slightly looser and more open, back of tongue slightly lower.
aught	[ɔ:t]	[ɔ:]	Lips more open but still rounded, back of tongue lower.

*The duration of Standard English vowels varies according to stress and context, but some vowels are normally of short duration while others are usually found in practice to be longer. Here the longer vowels are marked [:].

of	[ɒv]	[ɒ]	Lips retain very slight rounding, back of tongue lower.
father	['fɑ:ðə]	[ɑ:]	Lips relaxed and fully open, tongue at its flattest.
must	[mʌst]	[ʌ]	Lips stay relaxed, tongue humps slightly in centre.
learn	[lɜ:n]	[ɜ:]	Lips relaxed, tongue at its most relaxed, is raised in centre.
again	[ə'gen]	[ə]	Lips relaxed, the tongue may be slightly lower in centre.
and	[ænd]	[æ]	Lips relaxed, front of tongue slightly raised in forward part of mouth.
then	[ðen]	[e]	Lips relaxed, tongue raised more in front.
bring	[b ɪŋ]	[ɪ]	Lips relaxed, tongue raised more in front.
tea	[ti:]	[i:]	Lips relaxed, tongue raised to its highest forward position.

American stage speech also includes the 'mid-Atlantic' [a] as in 'ask' [ask]. In Standard English this sound only occurs in diphthongs [aɪ] and [aʊ]; roughly, it is similar to the Yorkshire sound in 'brass', [b as]; the lips are relaxed and the front of the tongue is raised slightly less than for [æ]. The sounds [ɜ:] and [ə] in American English may be coloured by [ɹ]; they would then be represented by the symbols [ɝ] and [ɚ].

With the simple vowels, each has its own shape made by the tongue, the lips and the cheeks, and as long as the vowel is sustained this shape does not change. Normally the vowels are resonated principally in the mouth/throat resonator.

Compound vowels

Sometimes one vowel flows directly into another to make a compound vowel, and since each element in the compound has its own shape, the whole of the compound cannot be sustained.

Diphthongs

now	[naʊ]	[aʊ]
skuas	[skjʊəz]	[ʊə]
fly	[flaɪ]	[aɪ]
home	[həʊm]	[əʊ]
making	['meɪkɪŋ]	[eɪ]
their	[ðɛə]	[ɛə]
fierce	[fɪəs]	[ɪə]
noises	['nɔɪzɪz]	[ɔɪ]

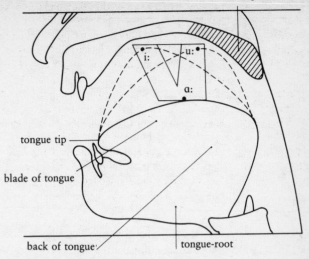

26 How the vowel charts relate to the mouth space

The dots on the vowel charts mark the highest point in the mouth space achieved by the tongue for the relevant vowel.

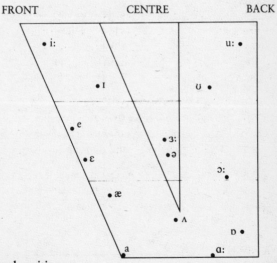

27 Vowel positions

Approximate highest positions of tongue for the English simple vowels

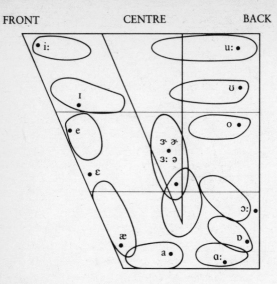

28   Vowel positions
Approximate positions of American vowels (American speech for the stage)

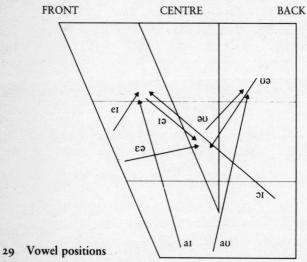

29   Vowel positions
Approximate movements of the
English diphthongs

American English has [ɑʊ] for [aʊ], [oʊ] for [əʊ] and, in addition, [ɔə] as in 'pour', [pɔəɹ], and [ɑə] as in 'car', [kɑəɹ].

Triphthongs

fire	[faɪə]	[aɪə]
power	[paʊə]	[aʊə]
player	[pleɪə]	[eɪə]
mower	[məʊə]	[əʊə]
lawyer	[lɔɪə]	[ɔɪə]

American English variants:
[ɑʊə] for [aʊə] and [oʊə] for [əʊə].

For a fuller description of the compound vowels see A. C. Gimson's *An Introduction to the Pronunciation of English* (Arnold).

Consonants

A consonant is a barrier formed by the organs of articulation to the breath-stream and it is important for clear speech that neither of the two forces involved – air-pressure and muscular barrier – is exaggerated (see The Vowel-Chain).

It is convenient for our purposes to divide the consonants into two main groups, those which have voice and those which are unvoiced.

Unvoiced			*Voiced*		
port	[pɔ:t]	[p]	bus	[bʌs]	[b]
			mum	[mʌm]	[m]
			wig	[wɪg]	[w]
fun	[fʌn]	[f]	vivid	['vɪvɪd]	[v]
thin	[θɪn]	[θ]	that	[ðæt]	[ð]
two	[tu:]	[t]	did	[dɪd]	[d]
sit	[sɪt]	[s]	zoo	[zu:]	[z]
			nun	[nʌn]	[n]
			love	[lʌv]	[l]
			doll	[dɒɫ]	[ɫ]
			muddle	[mʌdɫ]	[ɫ]
			{ run	[ɹʌn]	[ɹ]
			{ carriage	['kæɹɪdʒ]	[ɹ]

Unvoiced			*Voiced*		
ship	[ʃɪp]	[ʃ]	measure	[ˈmeʒə]	[ʒ]
chew	[tʃuː]	[tʃ]	judge	[dʒʌdʒ]	[dʒ]
cot	[kɒt]	[k]	gut	[gʌt]	[g]
			you	[juː]	[j]
			hang	[hæŋ]	[ŋ]
here	[hɪə]	[h]			

The voiced consonants, with the possible exception of those which have an explosive quality, use less breath than the unvoiced consonants; this is because during their formation the breath-stream has already met the barrier of the vocal cords. But in making the unvoiced consonants the breath-stream arrives with the consequences we have noted (see The Vowel-Chain, p. 126).

During the formation of some of the consonants, the breath-stream is completely stopped and then released, more or less explosively:

$$[p, b, k, g, t, d, tʃ, dʒ]$$

These consonants are particularly liable to over-tension during their formation. When this happens, too much air is expelled during the release which causes the following vowel to be breathy. The louder you are speaking, the more likely this effect.

Exercises

Introduction

After you have worked through the few tests and exercises which are provided here, you should have a good idea of your particular speech weaknesses, if you have any, and you can assimilate the necessary corrective work into your daily routine until they no longer present any problems. The exercises which follow are for guidance and are not meant to be comprehensive in scope; we begin with the mechanics of speech, limbering the muscles of the face and mouth; then there is a sequence of various syllables to test for facility of utterance with various conjunctions of sounds in various rhythms; after this we pass on to ordinary connected speech in the paragraphs, each of which concentrates on one or two consonants or vowels and which have to be read for sense as well as for articulatory precision; then, with the limbering done, we pass on to the work for which all of this is only a preparation – realizing the communicative intention.

Before you begin the speech work, make sure your voice is working well; pay great attention to keeping your good use functioning. Some speech sounds may prove difficult and provoke a tightening of the neck and a disruption of your breathing; this has to be inhibited; any unnecessary tension in the face or the speech organs must be released so that the speech sounds can be formed accurately but with the minimum of fuss. To get you going and to help release the jaw, perform the Whispered 'Ah' a couple of times; then try a few Vowel-Chains and keep the resonance full and balanced; the volume is not too important at this moment, but the quality of resonance is very important and is a guide to the effectiveness of your release and the state of your control in tuning and breathing.

Preparing the speech organs

The jaw

Take a few moments to check that you have your directions working and then, leaving the lips and tongue quite free, allow the jaw to open until you can comfortably insert a couple of fingers between the teeth; this is a wider opening than you will use most of the time in speech, but when you come to the speech work you should feel that this preparation has helped to remind you *where* you need to be free for the movements the jaw will make as you are speaking. A good idea at this stage is to let the jaw opening develop into a yawn – but keep the neck free as you do it.

The lips

1 Leave the teeth apart so that you can easily put a thumb knuckle between them, leave the tongue calm and slowly close the lips over the open teeth until a firm contact has been made; release and open the lips leaving the jaw free and still. Repeat this, gradually increasing speed. Breathe through the nose for this exercise.

2 Now try alternately lifting the bottom lip to the top lip and then bringing the top lip down to the bottom lip, allowing the lips to

rest apart between each movement. This will be quite a difficult stretch for the top lip and not everyone will be able to manage the full closure of the lips performed in this way; that doesn't much matter; merely trying to do it will help in the overall business of increasing agility in the speech organs and will help develop a better control of the lip movements.

3 Now, still keeping the jaw and tongue free but still, make a rapid series of openings and closings, moving both lips to meet at the mid-point of the opening between the teeth: if the meeting of the lips is firm enough, as you open them there will be a slight popping sound.

4 Now move the lips into a wide grin, still with the teeth apart and the tongue still, and then bring the lips together and pouting forward; do this rapidly a number of times aiming for a wider grin and a tighter pout each time.

5 With the lips together, but loosely, and with the teeth still apart, blow between the lips until you make a controlled and rapid vibration.

6 To finish this series of exercises, keep the lips closed and move the jaw downwards and forwards till it is as open as you can manage; keep the tongue free and untensed in the bottom jaw. This exercise should be performed slowly and carefully while you make sure the jaw doesn't tighten and the neck stays free.

The tongue

1 The jaw is released in the normal way and is open, the lips are open but untensed; now let the tongue-tip rest lightly against the bottom front teeth, breathe out through the mouth and place a finger under the jaw to check that the tongue-root is not tightening as you move the blade of the tongue easily, and at first slowly, between the position for making the vowel [ɑ:] and the position for [i:]. When you are sure that you can do this with the tongue-root and jaw free (there should be no movement of the jaw), gradually increase the speed of the tongue movement. Use a whisper to check the accuracy of your vowels.

2 Leave the lips and jaw open and stick the tongue-tip out so that it does not touch either the teeth or the lips; widen the tongue so

that the sides touch the inner corners of the lips; then narrow the tongue to a fine point. You may find that you wish to pull the tongue in and out of the mouth as you do this, but try to keep the tip out a *constant* distance – it need not be much, as long as it is forward of the lips. As you find you can perform these movements without tensing anything but the tongue, gradually build up speed.

3 Keep the pointed tongue-tip out and lightly and accurately make it touch in turn the centre of the top lip, the centre of the bottom lip, the centre of the hard palate, the left and right corners of the lips. Eventually you should be able to do this very fast. Breathe through the nose and leave the lips and jaw released all the time.

The cheeks

You may find it a help from time to time to give your face a gentle massage, particularly if unaccustomed work has made it ache. Do this with the finger-tips, and work each side of the face at the same time.

Place the finger-tips on the sides of the face, just under the cheek bones, and press lightly as you move the finger-tips in small circles, clockwise and anticlockwise; take this movement in towards the bridge of the nose, work down over the top lip, work the bottom lip and chin; end by stroking the sides of the face firmly up and down from the articulation of the jaw to the point of the chin. Leave the jaw free to move in response to the massage and keep the tongue free and at rest inside the mouth.

Muscular dissociation

One principle to keep firmly in mind as you perform these exercises is that you use the *simplest* movement, with the minimum effort, and this will mean practising muscular dissociation. Often when we move the lips we move the tongue, in sympathy as it were; or a tightening of the tongue may seem to call for a tightening of the neck or a twitch of the scalp; perhaps we find when we want to make a movement of the tip of the tongue that the whole tongue wants to tense. These sympathetic movements are not usually necessary and if we wish to have control of the organs of articulation we need to be able to dissociate one movement from another. A particularly obvious example of an unhelpful sympathetic movement would be that of closing the jaw when we only need to close the lips; if we do this we impair the fullness of resonance. I am not arguing here for the jaw to be fixed open, come what may; but the jaw should be *free* enough to be open even if the lips are closed.

Force is useless in the practice of muscular dissociation; the way to go about achieving it is to use the technique of stopping the habitual response, and to go about the business slowly and with thought, because breaking the pattern of muscular association is changing a habit of use. As control builds, we can perform the actions more quickly and with more or less strength as the rhythm of our speech demands, but always in a state of freedom and without pushing for a speedy result which may end up by getting us tied in knots.

Testwork syllables

Introduction

Now comes the time to test your articulation and to see whether any of the vowels and consonants present you with problems. Most of the problems we associate with speech are probably voice problems, and once the breathing and phonation is sorted out and working well these problems will disappear.

Lack of clarity which occurs because the speech is too muscular will disappear once the energy is centred in the vowel and the jaw is allowed to stay free so that the tongue can also be free to make light, deft movements.

Imprecision in the making of speech sounds, which leads to blurred articulation, is often the result of a local difficulty. In other words, you may be able to pronounce the individual sounds perfectly clearly by themselves, but when some sounds are placed in conjunction with other sounds, or when they are presented in an awkward rhythmic context, suddenly they become difficult to say.

Sometimes, too, imprecision in the articulatory movements occurs because the mobile speech organs (tongue, soft palate, lips) and the lower jaw are not accustomed to making precise and clear movements; perhaps the need for such movements has not been felt by the speaker in his ordinary conversation.

These are all quite ordinary problems and may be solved by applying the basic principles of efficient speech production and by practising the shaping of the sounds until control has been achieved; other, more serious speech defects, may have to be dealt with differently, and I shall make suggestions later.

Systematically work your way through the sounds and make as many different conjunctions as possible and with as many rhythmic variations as you can contrive. Eventually you will be left with a few groupings of vowels and consonants which you find difficult to pronounce clearly at speed; these are the sounds which need further practice and the others may be safely left. In practising the problem sounds, try to find words and phrases in which they occur and make up jingles and sentences, short and easy to memorize, and make a practice of repeating these in different rhythms and at different speeds until you find they are easy to say, and don't get in the way of full resonation.

Remember to keep the jaw free, to keep the neck free and your directions working, and to concentrate the speech energy in the flow of vowels. The moment that you feel the muscles of the organs of articulation are over-tightening or that they begin to ache, stop, release; and start again only after you have taken care to stop the tendency to strain.

Vowels

Simple rules:
1 The teeth never close for the vowels.
2 The mouth space is kept as large as practicable.
3 When the tongue rises for the front vowels there's no need for the lips to move.
4 Normally the soft palate is raised.
5 The root of the tongue is free at all times (use the ball of the thumb to check).

Start the practice by sustaining:

[ɑ:, e:, i:, ɑ:]
[u:, ɔ:, ɜ:, u:]

As you sustain each vowel, move the pitch around as if you were using the one sound only to say a whole phrase. Put a finger to the lips to make sure the breath spill is minimal, and at the same time check the tongue root is free.

Take the vowels of a phrase and join them in a chain:

[aʊ ‿ 'ɑː ‿ uː]

how <u>are</u> you?

Choose different phrases with different rhythms so the tune is well varied.

Switch rapidly from front vowels to back vowels, still checking that the tongue-root is free and the breath spill minimal:

[uː→iː, iː→ɒ, ɔː→e, ɑː→iː, æ→ʊ]

Vowels and consonants

The examples below are meant to exploit the following differences between types of syllable:

1 Where a syllable begins with a vowel: 'each', [iːtʃ]
2 Where it begins with a consonant: 'pea' [piː]
3 Where there is a vowel between consonants: 'peach' [piːtʃ]
4 Where the syllable is stressed in a group of syllables while the others remain unstressed: '<u>ga</u>thering', ['gæðəɹɪŋ], 'ap<u>pro</u>val', [ə'pɹuːvɫ], 'ciga<u>rette</u>', [sɪɡə'ɹet]

In practice it helps to shift the major stress around in a group to see if you still keep clear pronunciation as the rhythm changes:

['iːpipipi,   i'piːpipi,   ipi'piːpi,   ipipi'piː]

It is worth noting that difficulties of pronunciation which are caused by awkward rhythmic placing of a sound are more likely to occur when there is a cluster of unstressed syllables than when the stresses are fairly evenly shared out.

The unvoiced consonants

General rule: keep the air-pressure on the consonantal barrier to a practicable minimum, and don't allow the sound to become too breathy or too much air to leak away.

[s] and [ʃ] will need some approximation of the teeth, and probably so will [tʃ], but remember to keep the hinge of the jaw free and the back of the mouth open for vowel production.

For [f] remember to let the lower lip reach toward the top teeth, rather than having to close the jaws to make the speech-shape.

For [θ] remember to allow the tongue-tip to reach up to the top teeth rather than having to close the jaws.

Now, using the variations of syllable (1–4) we can build a framework for exploring the consonants; and use any other variations you care to invent as well:

[ɑːf, ɔːf, uːf, æf, iːf]
[fɑː, fɔː, fuː, fæ, fiː]
[ˈfɑːfɑː, ˈfɔːfɔː, ˈfuːfuː, ˈfæfæ, ˈfiːfiː]
[fːɑˈfɑː, fɔːˈfɔː, fuːˈfuː, fæˈfæ, fiːˈfiː]

And so with the other unvoiced consonants:
[p, θ, s, t, ʃ, tʃ, k, h]

Add consonants to the basic syllable and try it in different rhythms with different vowels – use the diphthongs as well:

[kɑː, kɑːf, kɑːfs, kɑːfθs]
[paɪ, paɪp, spaɪ, spaɪk, spaɪkθ, spaɪʃk]

It doesn't matter that these are for the most part nonsense sounds. Since they're not attached to meaning, it makes it easier to feel and hear what's going on.

Try, without forcing, always to let the jaw rest open, even for [s], [ʃ] and [tʃ] while you are saying the syllables; but don't let the jaw *fix* open; a practical opening would normally allow you to put a thumb knuckle between the teeth.

Vary the order of vowels and consonants and bring them into various conjunctions, but, for the moment, only using the unvoiced consonants. If you can pronounce a tortuous group such as [ˈtʃɪtʃɪstə] and still keep the voice well resonated *and* the consonants clear, you are well on the way.

The voiced consonants

Again the jaw may be left open for most of the voiced consonants. Only [z] needs approximation of the teeth although it is probably convenient for [ʒ] and [dʒ] as well; but as you practise these sounds in various syllabic formations, don't force the teeth apart; stop the joint of the jaw from tightening and concentrate on allowing the vowel-shape to dominate as you join sound to sound, syllable to syllable.

Most likely, since the jaw is free, it will move to close and open, but if you allow the proper degree of stretch in the tongue and the lips for the appropriate sounds, you will not *need* to close the jaw.

Don't be in a hurry or you might begin to force things; and you will probably find that you have to practise some degree of muscular dissociation if you are used to closing the jaw to make most of the consonants, because freeing the jaw to remain open when it is possible should not have the effect of over-relaxing the speech muscles which must still shape the consonants firmly, lightly and clearly.

With the voiced consonants there should be very little spilling of air as most of it is tuned into voice, but as you practise syllables with the voiced consonants, put a finger in front of your lips to see if there is airspillage. If there is, either the muscular effort in the organs of articulation is too strong or you are not tuning well. However, when you are testing for this escape of air, do not hold your breath; the object is to tune the air-flow not stop it.

When you have ensured that the resonance is good and the consonants are clear, you can mix voiced and unvoiced consonants in making your syllabic groupings. Again, keep the voice full and well produced.

Practice paragraphs

Each paragraph concentrates on one sound. I have given more attention to the consonants than the vowels because it's the consonants which tend to get in the way of good resonation. In the consonant paragraphs I have tried to bring the consonant under examination into conjunction with most of the vowel sounds and this has resulted in some odd story-lines and odder phrasing. However, despite the constant repetition of one sound in each of the paragraphs, they are not meant to be treated as tongue twisters. Read them aloud and tell the stories as simply and clearly as you can.

After the three paragraphs for nasal consonants, the paragraphs are ordered so that you work from the front of the mouth towards the back. This has no particular significance. Work on the paragraphs you find difficult and ignore the others.

After the consonant paragraphs come those for the vowels. These are kept short deliberately. Their usefulness will emerge when you are working on accents and want a sentence or two for each of the vowels to test the differences between your own vowels and those of the accent you are learning (see Working on Accents, pp. 189–92).

The nasal consonants

For a detailed explanation of how these consonants are formed and used in nasal resonation see the section Nasality and Nasal Resonance, pp. 86–90.

[m]

Maud and Mary Orme meandered arm in arm along the mosaic pavements of the museum and marvelled: monuments whose marmoreal magnificence reminded them of Mycenae, of Agamemnon and the Myrmidons; the tomb of a Ramessid – they exclaimed in amazement – the mummy of the man seemed almost immune to the damaging effect of time; on a screen from Matsumoto the moon loomed immense and calm over plum blossom and mountains swam in mist; in the gem room, tourmaline, diamonds, amber and amethyst and enamelled medallions gleamed; so many, so much to marvel at. 'Home,' moaned Mary, 'I'm moithered and lame for life. I've such a mad mix of images swimming in my mind I'm sure I'll dream I'm imprisoned in this museum and wake up screaming.' 'Mary,' Maud remonstrated mildly, 'we've one more room to view.' 'No, Maud, my mind's made up!' Mary and Maud went home – to malted milk and muffins.

[n]

The Nine Nuns, a northern Scandinavian gang of feminist anarchists, by now known to Interpol and urgently wanted for snatching ten Benin bronzes from an important collection in Nineveh, were apprehended in the end at dawn on the dunes near Sandwich landing from canoes. They'd changed their appearance and strange garments indicated they were meant to be taken for English nannies on vacation. Their prawn-nets and

knitting and brown knee-length stockings didn't take in Euan
McNab, the senior constable present, when he noted their
handbags contained none of the equipment nannies need and are
known for: needles, buttons, bananas, iodine, nailbrushes and
ribbons – and the Nine Nuns were all wearing nacre nail varnish.

[ŋ]

A Frank, what are you doing?

B Drawing.

A Not 'King Kong conquers the Mongolians' again?

B No, some punk monks with their tongues sticking out.

A Will you be long?

B I'll just work out the angles of their ankles – the gown gives
problems with monks – and then get in their cinctures. You
could bring gin, glasses and ice and we'll have some tinctures.
Thanks.

A How are we at the bank? I've a hankering for some dangly ear-
rings and matching bangles.

B What length ear-rings?

A So they swing and tinkle when I fling my head about.

B Ah, you're looking at my monks – what do you think?

A What I'm seeing and what you're drawing are two different
things.

B They're singing.

A I think I'll have that drink.

The front consonants

[p] and [b]. For these consonants the lips close firmly over the open
jaw and care should be taken that the teeth do not come together
needlessly. The explosion as the lips release is firm and a slight puff
of breath will be felt on a finger held to the lips; this should be kept
as economical as possible.

[p]

Percy's my pet and no mere pig but a properly plump porcine
prince of prodigious pedigree and poise. His principal post-
meridional repast is porridge, pease pottage and pickled pistachios
with, for pudding, pineapple pastries permeated with pastis. For
supper, to keep up his powerful poundage, he prefers apples – but
spits out the pips – potato-peel and scraps of paper splashed with

pear pulp and topped with raspberry lollipops. No pig can compare
with peerless Percy. But keeping him's a problem – cooped up in
his pen he peaks and pines and gawps at the open pasture where
Petronella, his spouse, and their piglets, the perfect products of
their passionate propagation, sport by the pool. Poor Percy, poor
Petronella – poorest of the poor their piglets: predestined for the
chopper; then, pork chops for the shopper, one and all.

[b]

Barbara Boydell's bonkers again. Her bees have all got foulbrood,
Biggleswade bombilates with bad bumble bees and all
Bedfordshire might soon be beset. Poor Babs; she sits in her
burberry and bobble hat in her arbour – beehives before her,
elderberry bushes behind – smoking her hubblebubble to keep the
bluebottles at bay and imbibing barley wine from a barrel by her
elbow. There, brooding on the improbable behaviour of her bees,
she's becoming babbling bibulous on the beer. Barely
comprehensible, she sobs: 'Boy oh boy, Barbara, you've really
boobed!' Bashing her bosom she burbles 'The blossom's on the
bough – but no bees buzzing about their business! What about the
crab apple, borage and balsam, the bloody rhubarb, you
abominable bees? What about the butterbeans and beetroot?' She
grabs the barrel and absorbs. Then, half blotto and quite barmy,
Barbara the bee-bore goes back to her boorish brooding – for all
the world like Buddha under his Baobab.

[w] is often called a semi-vowel; it has the lip shape of [u:] but the
tongue position varies according to the vowel which follows. It is
voiced, and care must be taken not to allow an unvoiced breathy
quality into the sound even when it is preceded by [k], as in 'quiet',
[kwaɪət]. Again, the teeth are left well apart.

[w]

When the choir went to watch the woodworker, Wabash
Wedgwood, Wendell Worsley and Wilma Wauchope squabbled
in whispers and quarrelled in squeaks all the way until we were
weary. But Wabash welcomed us to his workshop waggling a
wicked-looking weapon for woodcarving and quelled them with
a word: 'Quiet in the choir!' he requested. 'Wow!' said Wilma
weakly and waddled, swaying, away to one side where she leaned

swooning against a wall, looking waxy and wheyfaced. At once,
Wendell whipped off his windcheater and began wafting it over
her. 'What's the matter?' he questioned, 'would you like some
water? Wake up Wilma you've gone all wishy-washy!' Whereupon
Wilma awoke: 'Why Wendell, you're worried; now why's that,
I wonder?' 'I worship you, Wilma' replied her woebegone wooer,
awkwardly, still wafting away. The choir left them to it and we
wandered after Wabash to wonder at his exquisite workmanship;
and even more at that queerly quarrelsome couple, Wilma and
Wendell.

[f] and [v] are made by vibrating the airstream between the bottom
lip and the top teeth. Care must be taken to allow the bottom lip to
stretch to the teeth so that the jaws may remain apart.

[f]

My fine-fettled but ferocious friend Frank feeds on fritters and
frequently frightens my fluffier friend Fifi into fainting fits. When
Frank's foul and fierce, fainting always follows. Especially when
Frank offers Fifi his dreadful fritters for she's frightened of getting
fat (she's got a fairly full figure already). What a kerfuffle when
Fifi foolishly offers Frank falafel for breakfast instead of fritters!
Frank goes all fierce, Fifi falls off the sofa, the falafel falls to the
floor and I fall about laughing. Falafel football follows with Fifi
shrieking 'Foul! Unfair!' as she attempts to foil Frank's left-footers
at the by now filthy falafel. We all finish breakfasting with Frank's
fritters – or gefüllte fish if it's offered. If you have to visit Frank or
Fifi, refuse the food – it's all frightful.

[v]

Vercingetorix was a vast aardvark, vociferously virile but
invariably vacuous and vague. (He'd been vivisected and then
revivified, but that was for varicose veins). He averred a perfervid
passion for velvety Violet, the vole with the voluptuous voice
and vigorous uvula. Unavailing. 'Move over, Vercingetorix;
revolve, you vapid vertebrate,' snapped the vivacious vole evilly
as the cavorting aardvark gave vent to his volcanic and vulnerable
love in volumes of convoluted verse; 'the view would improve if
you would vacate it, Aardvark.' Devastated, Vercingetorix
absolved Violet of her viciousness, vowed to preserve his virginity

for ever and left for Vladivostok on his velocipede. Now he's the only vodka-swilling aardvark with a vasectomy.

[ð] and [θ] are made by passing the airstream between the raised tongue-tip and the top front teeth. Care must be taken that there is no airspill over the sides of the tongue, which will give a slushy imprecision to the sounds. The teeth are apart for this sound, though the resulting stretch of the tongue might make you feel uncomfortable at first. Keep the jaw free and make sure the airstream is well supported.

[ð]

'Bother! *And* other oaths!' mouthed my mother's father's brother Boothby as the soap got up his nose. He was bathing, and breathed with difficulty as, wreathed with steam and smothered with suds, he scythed the lathered stubble on his weathered, leathery old face with a cut-throat razor. Seething pink, though lithe in his unclothed condition, here and there he flung the offending suds, and hither and thither they splattered. 'These thy thighs are too thin, thou worthy Boothby, and thy shanks are shrunk withal. Lathe-spindly – like that – they are' he pointed to a chair with the cut-throat; and thus he apostrophized, and with this sank the withered objects deep.

[θ]

Bertha Theakstone, pathologist, earthmother with a thick wreath of hair, mammoth of girth and thew, and forthright in her enthusiasms, at thirty-three grew breathless at the thought of Arthur Guthrie the thistle-thin Leith mathematician. Though he was toothless and loathsome of breath, she'd thirsted for him ever since that Thursday in Woolworth when he'd thrust a polyanthus upon her. How thunderously her heart had thudded in her thorax as she'd thanked him: 'How thoroughly couth!' and, her voice ethereal with pathos, 'Arthur you're the flame to my moth!' 'It's not worth thinking about, Bertha, the thing's just a polyanthus.' Thwarted and thankless her passion, she thinned to a wraith reading his books: 'Guthrie's Authentic Method for Confounding Theologians with Mathematics', 'Thirty More Atheistical Theories from a Ruthless Anti-Catholic'. Thin as a

lath she went south to her sister Ethel and now lives in Thanet.
The polyanthus thrives despite both of them.

The middle consonants

[s] and [z] are capable of two formations. In the first, which is
normal English usage, the tongue-tip is raised towards the alveolar
ridge, the sides of the tongue seal against the top teeth and the
airstream is directed down a narrow channel in the centre of the
tongue; the noise of the airstream passing between the tongue-tip
and the alveolar ridge and hitting the teeth makes the [s], and when
voice is added, the [z]. The second form allows the tongue-tip to be
at rest behind the bottom front teeth and the [s/z] is made as the air
passes over the raised blade of the tongue; the sides of the tongue
seal with the top teeth as for the first shape.

The faults most frequently met with are:

1 the tongue-tip is allowed too far forward and a sound between
   [s] and [θ] or [z] and [ð] is made – the lisp; the remedy is to
   practise keeping the tongue-tip back well clear of the teeth.

2 A sharply hissing [s] may be produced when the air-pressure is
   great and the aperture between tongue-tip and alveolar ridge too
   small; the remedy is to sustain the [s], release the pressure of the
   tongue-tip gradually, and move the tongue-tip back a fraction.
   As you move the tongue-tip forward the note will rise, as you
   move it back, the note will drop. To aid the general resonance of
   the voice it helps if the [s/z] position is such that the [s] sounds
   fairly low and the tongue-tip is not unduly tensed.

3 A lateral [s/z], which has elements of [ʃ/ʒ] in it and sounds slushy;
   this can often be remedied by working from [t] and [d]; the [t/d]
   is made in the ordinary way, with the sides of the tongue sealing
   with the upper teeth and the tip pressed lightly to the mid-part
   of the alveolar ridge; as the tip is released, slowly and gently, and
   the air allowed to pass over the tongue-tip, the [s/z] is heard
   clearly – providing the sides of the tongue have not been allowed
   to move, and the tongue-tip has not dropped too far. In any
   event, to avoid the lateral spillage of air, you must work gently
   and patiently to achieve a good seal between the sides of the
   tongue and the top teeth.

One point to remember when working on [s], if you are to avoid making it over-sibilant, is that the energy is still directed towards the voice-stream. This has the effect of minimizing the [s] and helps keep the jaw free. This is important with both [s] and [z] which, more than any other sounds, demand the jaws to be close together. The looser the jaw and the more open the resonating space the better, both for the voice and for [s] and [z].

[s]

Simon Sassoon is easily seasick and stands at the stern of the SS *Sassafras* staring dizzily downwards towards the greasily seething aqueous substance below. The sibilant susurration of the sea as it hisses and sucks at the sides of the ship and swells past towards the Sussex shore seems seriously distressful to Simon – as if steel is insufficiently substantial to withstand the endless relentlessness of surge and suction. He is sensible he's too susceptible to the suggestive sight of the slick slimy scum on the wake as it slips and slides past. A spasm seizes his stomach as he suppresses the desire to be sick. 'This stuff's serviceable for fishes, cetaceans and seahorses,' he dismally and supercilliously supposes, 'but most decent species stay on shore.' Thus he dismisses the sea. He despises the first sailors for their restless insistence on searching the seas – Pacific, Caspian, Sargasso – even the Solent – 'so silly,' he whispers miserably to himself. The breeze changes; diesel smuts from the exhaust stream past his sensitive nose. Simon Sassoon zigzags unsteadily towards the stairs, seeking the saloon and some whisky to sustain his sinking spirits on this nightmarish crossing.

[z]

A Zacharias, whose is the zither with the zigzags?

B Zebedee's.

A D'you suppose I could use it for the Xenophobe's gigs?

B Easily. As long as Zebedee doesn't get wise to it.

A It'd be crazy with the xylophone – some music!

B Sounds zany, Zuleika.

A Zebedee uses his zither a lot, doesn't he?

B Zip up, Zuleika, I'm musing. Don't make noises – it unpoises me.

A Was I? Sorry. Well, I'll ease off with the zither. My car's outside.

B Zoomy. Now buzz off. You've exhausted even my amazing
   patience. I hope the Xenophobes get good houses and you
   really zonk them with the zither and xylophone, but close the
   doors *behind* you, would you, please?

[ʃ] and [ʒ] are formed as the airstream passes over the blade of the
tongue which is raised towards the alveolar ridge; the sides of the
tongue seal with the back top teeth; (the tip is relaxed away from
the palate and rests behind the bottom teeth); the aperture through
which the breath-stream passes is larger than for [s/z] and consequently the sound is less pressurized; the lips may be rounded
slightly for these sounds, depending to some extent on the context.
[ʃ] and [ʒ] may suffer from similar faults to those encountered with
[s] and [z]. Usually, when [s] and [z] have been corrected the [ʃ] and
[ʒ] will sound better too. The teeth may be well apart for these
sounds if the jaw is properly released.

[ʃ]

Shrieks and shrill imprecations from the washhouse showed Sasha
that Sheila, her sluggish flat-sharer had suffered a shock. 'Show
me, Sheila,' she sighed; and she did: 'See!' she shouted, 'my
Egyptian shift has shrunk to a shirt!' 'That's a shame,' said Sasha
unemotionally, 'surely you shouldn't've machine-washed it. Now
hush, Sheila,' she cautioned, 'these shrieks are too shaming.'
'Shut up,' snarled Sheila, splashing washing everywhere. 'This is
sheer foolishness, Sheila, I wish . . .' Whoosh! a shoe shied by
Sheila shot past Sasha's shoulder and shattered a pitcher of shoyu
on a shelf. No shilly-shallying for Sasha; her eyes flashing Russian
passion, she sharply shied the shoe right back so it splashed the
washing, and Sheila, most efficiently with shoyu. And thus the
wretched shrieker got short shrift from Sasha over her shrunk
shift.

[ʒ]

A Is it an explosion?
B I suppose that was an allusion to my latest collage.
A Well, that casualty in the embrasure.
B Thank you. A remark I shall treasure.
A It's most unusual. There's even a measure of occasional
   pleasure to be had from it I suppose.

B   If one has the leisure to observe the precision of my vision.

A   What's it called? 'Collision'?

B   'Beige Peugeot, Bruges.' As a result of what you so casually
    called a collision, the car is suffering from a profusion of lesions
    and contusions, its engine has had a seizure leading to
    implosion, and, due to over-exposure, corrosion has
    occurred.

A   My word!

B   Here it's in the Car Massage Parlour . . .

A   Oh I thought that was a garage.

B   Well it's both. The Asian in the azure blazer is a nurse, and
    he's making the decision whether or not to make provision
    for an oil-transfusion. You see?

A   With some confusion.

B   Essentially my vision is that the division between the
    mechanical and the human is illusion: once the car was an
    intrusion but now we live in symbiotic fusion.

A   Now I see: not so much 'Collision' as 'Collusion'.

[tʃ] and [dʒ], as their phonetic symbols suggest, have some of the
qualities of [t] + [ʃ] and [d] + [ʒ]. The tongue-tip is raised to the
alveolar ridge causing a blockage of the air-flow which must not be
allowed to leak away sideways – and to stop this, the sides of the
tongue seal with the back top teeth, but at slightly less pressure than
for [ʃ] or [ʒ]. The release of the tongue-tip from the alveolar ridge
causes a gentle explosion of the air which makes the sound [tʃ] and,
when voice is added, [dʒ].

   Again, making these sounds sometimes seems easier if the teeth
are close together. This is to be avoided. The body of the tongue is
retracted for [ʃ] and [ʒ], [tʃ] and [dʒ], and any closure of the jaw
seriously interferes with resonation – more so than closed jaws
would interfere with the resonation of [m] for example. So, again,
keep the jaw free and the voice-stream well supported.

[tʃ]

There will be chanting, and chimes from the church bells, when
Archibald and Charmian Chichester's urchin, Charles, is
christened in the village church of Chawdle-under-Cheaterham
on Tuesday. The choir (under adventurous Christian

Cholmondeley, the chutney manufacturer, the chap whose
achievements with the choir are unquestionable) will be in
cheerful tuneful action for young Charles. Afterwards there will
be a choice of cheese and chutney sandwiches or chops to chew
on, chowder or poached roach to choke on, champagne and
Chablis to drink. The guests will perch wretchedly on chairs and
chesterfields in the Chichesters' charming cottage, in picturesque
postures, munching their chops and chives or apples from the
orchard. They'll catch each others' eye and chatter about literature,
the changeability of the weather, the choosiness of Charmian, and
how Archibald drops his aitches.

[dʒ]

Mr Justice St John Jermyn, the judge, decided to adjourn for lunch
and urged the journalists engaged on the case not to badger the
witnesses and the jury. Jammed in the dock, James Gillson the
giant gemologist, John Hodgkins, the Geordie jewel thief, and
heavily jowled George Jewison, Major-General, retired (late of
the Royal Engineers), were jointly charged with perjury. The
foreman of the jury, Eugene Jones, a hedge and verge cutter, edged
towards his neighbour and nudged him gently: 'That General
won't enjoy porridge* at his age, Jack,' he murmured. 'I don't
enjoy it much at mine,' was Jack's rejoinder.

[t] and [d] are shaped somewhat according to the sounds they lie
next to. The simple form of [t] and [d] as in the jingle:

       Ten tiny toads came tumbling into town

    Where a dozen dirty dogs were dashing up and down

is formed by lifting the tongue-tip to the alveolar ridge to block the
air-flow, then the tongue-tip is released and there is a mild explosion
as the airstream continues. To avoid too much air escape at the
moment of plosion, the tongue-tip is placed lightly on the alveolar
ridge, the less muscular pressure the better. A common fault with
[t] and [d] is to place the tongue-tip against the teeth, or too far
forward on the alveolar ridge; this gives a thin spitting sibilance to
the sounds.

    The dental [t/d] occurs when the [t] or [d] comes before [θ] or [ð]

---

*Slang for time spent in prison. Jack takes the word in its normal sense – oatmeal.

(as in 'whi<u>te</u>thorn' and 'an<u>d th</u>en'); it is normal for the tongue to assume the shape of [θ] or [ð] but with the added pressure of the [t/d] transferred from the alveolar ridge to the top teeth so there is a stoppage of the air-flow which is released into the [θ] or [ð].

The [t/d] with nasal plosion occurs with [t] or [d] before [n] or [m] (as in 'mu<u>tt</u>on' and 'su<u>dd</u>en', 'pos<u>tm</u>aster' and 'a<u>dm</u>inistration'). Some speakers prefer to pronounce the [t] separately but this has an over-careful feel to it. The [t/d] is held and the plosive release is made into the nose as the soft palate drops for the nasal consonant.

The [t/d] with lateral plosion occurs when [t] or [d] is followed by a sustained 'l', [ɫ] (as in 'fe<u>ttle</u>' and 'a<u>ddle</u>'). The tongue-tip is raised in the normal way but the release of the stopped airstream is made across the sides of the tongue; the tip stays sealing with the alveolar ridge until the [ɫ] is finished. The main fault with these sounds is likely to be the premature release of the tongue-tip, thus making a normal [t/d] separate from [ɫ].

The post alveolar [t/d] occurs when [t] or [d] is followed by [ɹ] (as in 't<u>ry</u>' and 'd<u>ry</u>'). Anticipation of the [ɹ] causes the tongue-tip to curl back to seal with the palate just behind the alveolar ridge. The [t] + [ɹ] or [d] + [ɹ] are thus shaped simultaneously at the moment when the tongue-tip releases the blocked airstream. These sounds are likely to make you want to close the jaws; there is normally no need to do this, though some slight movement of the jaw is normal. Listen to the quality of the resonance flow and if you seem to be getting a thin sound after [dɹ] or [tɹ], try leaving the teeth more apart; maintain jaw release throughout.

[t]

> He was taught as a tot to toot on his flute
> While his mother tut-tutted and tatted.
> The tits in the trees
> Took tight hold in the breeze,
> Tête-à-tête with the tooter they chatted.

MacOuart the agriculturalist put together his report as he tucked into hot tea, buttered toast and strawberry tarts. He tonged sugar into his teacup, stirred – and stopped, tapping the table-top. The heart of the matter was targets: had they been bettered or not? The beetroots bitter, potatoes late, oats eaten by goats, stands of mustard laid flat by torrents of rain, and tares in the wheat – the tally was terrible, the picture not pretty at all. He turned to livestock. Trout tremendous and tasting great, steers fat, goats fatter – outright laughter was not his style but he tittered at the thought of the goats. Loitering over his tea he totalled it up. Not too bad. He tipped back his seat and took yet another toothsome tart.

[d]

From dawn to dusk up hill and down dale, delivering dabs, daice and flounders, squid and daintily dappled trout, Dido the delivery donkey endeared herself to elderly rural residents in Devonshire from Dartmouth to Diddicombe. Her endurance passed into Devonian legend: her daredevil dash at dusk during December to deliver dogfish to the D'Oyley-Dankworths at Doone Dingle for their Friday dinner – and that despite a blizzard on Dartmoor; her deadly devotion to Dick Durden the wet fish dealer who owned and drove her until, in the end, she got doddery, was renowned. Then Dick did something so dotty and daft it defies description; he decided one deed more to distinguish her doughtiness among donkeys was called for and he entered Dido for the Devon Donkey and Dogcart Derby. Disaster. Dido did all she could do and dashed away with determination; but she dropped down dead in the dust, dragging her dog-cart behind her. Dido's doleful demise was deplored throughout Devon and Dick Durden, deeply downhearted, dived into a decline and followed his dear Dido within days.

> Here departed lies Dido the Donkey
> And Durden the Dealer in Fish
> He was the ass and she died Oh
> To grant him his last foolish wish.

[t] (dental)

Pat's heart-throb is put through it by Pat though he seems to enjoy it. 'Put that shirt to dry, it's wet through and get those socks off, too! Then eat this while it's hot.' 'Great thought, Pat, though not this morning. I'll eat the stew, but there's that whitethorn at the gate that I must thin, and an eighth of the garden I must think

about planting, then . . .' 'But then, those wet things.' 'But . . .'
'Then bed!' 'All right then,' he said.

[d] (dental)

'Have you tried this?' He offered Thea a drink in an old thin glass.
She remembered thinking weird thoughts, how odd the colour
was, red though not purple. And then again it seemed that many
colours swirled there. She remembered Thurston had asked that
she drink it sitting, but she'd stood there. 'What is it?' she asked
thickly, her tongue a dead thing in her mouth. Jud Thurston
laughed then. 'That's the last thing to ask – ask rather "is it a good
thing or a bad thing?" and then . . .' His voice faded through
thinning air. It seemed that the width and breadth of the room
had changed, that she was not there really, that . . . she dropped
the glass. 'You drugged that drink' she heard Thea say; and then
she watched Thea as she fell.

[t] (with nasal plosion)

As soon as it was curtains for Henry Wooten the cotton and button
potentate, Houghton Hall got a new owner. Interest mounted in
the village: who'd inherit an awful place like Houghton Hall?
Drayton did. 'A bit much, that nutcase Drayton,' Ayrton said,
'he oughtn't to eat nothing but mutton. And what on earth does
he do?' At the Goat and Compasses Brereton felt threatened: 'A
latent satanist – he gathers betony at night and there's a certain
moistness in his eyes . . . of course I couldn't be certain . . .' At
the Cat and Fiddle Bethune confessed himself beaten: '. . . so
spartan; oaten porridge and wheaten bread is all he's eaten – the
mutton's for his kittens.' A heightening and tightening of interest
was patent when the postmaster reported Drayton had put an
ad in his window: 'Wanted, part-time cook to fatten ten kittens
and a botanist.'

[d] (with nasal plosion)

The burden of modern behaviour weighed an awful lot on Riordan,
but he showed an admirable calm when the groundsman,
Cowden, suddenly confronted him at midnight with the
maddening news that hidden near the midden in the headmaster's
garden he'd found Dearden with the gardener's hoydenish
daughter Emily Weaden. 'I'd an idea they shouldn't be there, sir,'

said Cowden. Dearden had cleared an old wooden arbour in the rhododendrons, lured an unsuspecting Emily there and was saddening the maiden's ears with deadening talk of Auden and Haydn; and though she cared enormously for Dearden and had made an effort with Auden, she couldn't take Haydn and was gladdened by the entrance of Cowden, even though he'd trodden on her red nylon dirndl in the dark. Riordan decided an interview with Cowden, Dearden and the hoyden would only harden his arteries. 'We are ancient, they are modern – we must pardon them,' he said; and went to bed.

[t] (lateral plosion)

In the bar of the Skittle Whittler in Bootle, Stewart Piert'll chortle over his beer and dottle and tittle-tattle on about the near fatal battle between Myrtle Bartle and the cattleman on the vital question of what wheat'll do this year. Myrtle rattled the cattleman with the kettle, but he was soon on his mettle and sent her hurtling over the settle, which turned turtle. Myrtle beetled out screaming 'I'll fetch you a clout'll kill you!' and hit him with the coal skuttle. 'That'll do it!' he gasped, nettled, spittle and dental bits flying. 'That soot'll ruin my suit – Stewart'll bear witness and the Court'll do you for this. It'll be all up with you now Myrtle Bartle!' 'Hootle tootle,' responded Myrtle obscurely, 'you're mental – the cart'll pull the horse before that,' and picked up a bottle. The cattleman bolted.

[d] (with lateral plosion)

Meddling Mrs Myddleton needled the Beadle over his handling of the Bridlington Fair. 'It'll be Bedlam in the Saddlery! The crowd'll addle Cawdle's brains – he'll dawdle with the change, let the milk curdle and muddle up the strudel and the girdle cakes. What about the events in the middle tent? The Edelweiss Yodelling Competition again? That idle fellow McArdle'll win the medal, he always does, just as Waddell'll win the Bundle Trundle Over Hurdles.' The Beadle bridled: 'What about Dog Handling?' A poodle sidled into the room and Mrs Myddleton seized it bodily. 'Adlam's brindled Beddlington has had it; this year *I'm* entering with Fardel. He handles beautifully, don't you Fardel?' and she gave the poor poodle a punishing cuddle.

[t] (post alveolar)

Trotty Trubshaw's betrothal to the Eritrean was truly traumatic. An intruder tripped the outside alarm during the party. It transpired he was a truant tramp who'd strayed off the street. He was striving to retreat when he trod on a trowel and tangled with a rose-trellis attached to a tree trunk. Trembling with terror and treading on the trellis, which he destroyed, he was trickily trapped by the Eritrean, strongly trussed with his trouser belt and treated by Trotty to a lecture on the law of trespass while she fed him pastrami in pastry and truffled trifle.

[d] (post alveolar)

A Druce, your drawing of Droitwich is maladroit.

B How dreadful for you, Drury.

A There's a dragon in it!

B Yes – a poor bedraggled dribbling drabness of a dragon – he's called Driffield and he's dry as a drought.

A Droll. What's he doing in Droitwich?

B Dragging a dray and being driven by a drunkard dressed as a Druid; in the dray are drums of draft ale which the Druid and his dropout dragon will drain to the dregs to drown their sorrows.

A But why is Driffield the dropout dragon drawing a dray in Droitwich?

B I dreamed it.

A You were drunk. You're a drone and a drifter, Druce. Draco had laws for such as you. How could you draw a dragon in Droitwich?

A Because Droitwich, without Driffield, is so dreadfully dreary!

'r'

The symbol [ɹ] is here used to describe the fricative, and the alveolar tap. 'r' is found in three forms in the British Isles: The fricative as in 'red', the alveolar tap between vowels as in 'thorough', and the rolled Scots 'r'. The alveolar tap is hardly used at all by most Standard English speakers now, at any rate in ordinary conversation, its place having been taken by the fricative [ɹ]. However, if a particularly crisp diction is required it is quite useful. The fricative [ɹ] is formed by cupping the tongue-blade towards the alveolar ridge; the voiced airstream is vibrated between the tongue-tip and the forward part of the hard palate anterior to the alveolar ridge, or, at times, the ridge itself. The commonest fault with [ɹ] is the failure of the blade to rise and form the cup shape. Then a kind of 'w' is made instead with the lips playing an important part in the formation of the sound. This may sometimes be due to the tongue-string being too short to allow a sufficient curl back to the tongue blade; if this is the case [l/ɫ] will be affected as well. For practice it is advisable to attempt the fricative [ɹ] without sympathetic lip movements to ensure that the tongue-tip is working properly in making the sound.

In normal connected speech it is usual to pronounce the written 'r' when it can be used as a link into a word beginning with a vowel – although the written 'r' would not be pronounced before a break in speech or before a word beginning with a consonant. So 'come here' [kʌm hɪə], and 'here goes' [hɪə gəʊz], but 'here it is' [hɪəɹ‿ɪt ɪz].

On this analogy, quite often [ɹ] is made between a word which ends with a vowel and contains no written vowel and a word which begins with a vowel: 'Amanda‿r‿is', [ə'mændəɹ‿ɪz]; 'idea‿r‿of', [aɪ'dɪəɹ‿əv]. This is called the Intrusive 'r'. On the whole, for clarity, it is probably better not to use the Intrusive 'r' except in those common everyday phrases in which its use is no longer remarkable and where not to use it would sound over-precise and pedantic. This must be a matter of personal judgement and observation.

In Canada and the United States the 'r' may be continued into a following vowel and lend it coloration; so for 'error' we get ['eɹɚ] instead of Standard English ['eɹə]. This process has developed to the point where some vowels, with some speakers, take part of their intrinsic quality from the consonantal coloration, most notably [ɜ:] which becomes [ɝ] and [ə] which becomes [ɚ]; so for 'bird' we get [bɝd] (instead of Standard English [bɜ:d]). Characteristically, with this use the tongue is more retracted than for Standard English [ɹ], with the sides of the tongue in contact with the upper back teeth; in consequence there is often either a 'darker', fuller, back-of-the-mouth and throat resonation for the vowels, or, in some cases, considerable nasalization.

In general, in North American speech, if an 'r' occurs in the written form of the word it is pronounced. American speakers on the whole very seldom make the Intrusive 'r' – certainly far less frequently than Standard English speakers; there are some words where the Intrusive 'r' is made habitually by some speakers (for example [kɜ·nɫ], 'colonel'), possibly from analogy with a similar word where the 'r' is orthographic (in the case of 'colonel': 'kernel'), but more probably because the vowel is customarily pronounced with 'r' coloration.

[1]

Roy Ryder ran wretchedly round his rock garden ranting against rain. There was rain everywhere, in trickles and torrents. Unrestrained by the river courses, it ran in rivulets through the countryside creating strange creeks and runnels, ruining the root crops, deracinating trees in forests and rhododendrons in shrubberies – and thoroughly ravaging the rhubarb and radishes, and wrecking the red roses in Roy Ryder's rockery. Roy was really cross when the rain got his raspberries, but when it reached, and breached, his greenhouse and shrivelled his rare orchids, the air rang with strange, lurid oaths and terrible swearing. Then round and round he ran throwing drowned roses and rotten rhubarb everywhere, shrieking raucous horticultural profanities in the most reprehensible way. Reg Ruben, his neighbour, came across Roy cowering in his greenhouse dribbling and muttering shrill imprecations. 'Roy, this is irresponsible,' he remonstrated, 'this ranting and roaring against the rain. Read an interesting library book for relief, give yourself a literary treat for a change – after all, there's plenty more rhubarb around.' As Roy tried to throttle poor Reg, Reg realized his friend was too horribly angry for redemption through literature, and breaking free, he ran.

[l] (light 'l') and [ɫ] (dark or sustained 'l')

[l] is made by lifting the tongue-tip to the alveolar ridge and allowing the voice-stream to pass sideways around this obstruction, which is only made very briefly before the tongue-tip lowers; the body of the tongue holds the shape of the vowel which is to follow. [ɫ] is made somewhat similarly, but the body of the tongue holds the shape of the preceding vowel and the tongue-tip is held in contact with the alveolar ridge for longer than with [l]. Another difference is that in [l] the tongue-tip forms less of a cup in sealing with the

alveolar ridge than does the [ɫ]. Some Irish speakers use a continuing [l] in lieu of [ɫ] and to achieve the full [ɫ] need to bring the tongue-tip back a fraction, and make more of the upward stretch of the tongue-tip. If the tongue-string is too short to allow a proper lift of the tongue-tip, the [ɫ] will often be replaced by [ʊ] or [o].

The syllabic [ɫ], as formed with [t] and [d], has appropriate exercises under [t] and [d] with lateral plosion.

[l] and [ɫ]

Lalage Pilleau lurked by her loom, her labours halted, a pile of coloured wools on a stool by her angular elbow left coiled and tangled. She looked a miserable lump loitering there. She was reflecting on the cruelty of Carl Clark, her faithless lover, who'd left her for a lanky blonde model girl called Lil Bowles – or, professionally, Leila St Leger. Lonely and lovelorn, she mulled it all over. How Carl had lolled collarless and leering by the eel pool among the wild fennel, wholly careless of her feelings, and told her all the lurid details. 'She's luscious, Lal! Long legs, laughs a lot, likes a giggle over a glass, lives a wonderful life as a model – glamorous, you know – she's got flair, she likes liqueurs, not pale ale.' He'd scowled, 'So, Lal, it's all over for us; Lil's a girl in a million'. While the light lessened and grew gloomy around her loom, Lalage's lovely lips quivered and her eyelids trembled. She lowered her head and howled loudly for her latest lost love.

The back consonants

[j] is included with the back consonants because the further back in the mouth it is formed, the better for voice production. It is made by raising the tongue-blade near the hard palate and passing the voiced airstream through the narrow gap thus made. The more of the front of the tongue you can leave uninvolved in this action, the better. Great attention needs to be given to releasing the tongue-root for [j]. Use the ball of the thumb to check. No breath spill should be felt on a finger held on the lips. [j] is also described as a semi-vowel.

[j]

Yorick Yeames from Yare, the Yeats expert, and usurious Ursula Younghusband from Yeovil kept a yawl at Yarmouth and went for serious yacht trips every year. One year, together with Yum-

Yum Ure from Uist, the uraemia specialist, and her youthful Yankee boyfriend Uriah Yeomans from Yale – renowned for his yodelling and his yowling hound Yucatan – they opted for the great Yellow River. 'Europe, the Yemen and even Uruguay must yield to my yearning for the Yangtze Kiang!' yelled Ursula. 'Yonder,' said Yorick obligingly, 'lies the yawl; we've yoghurt and honey and millions of onions and, yes, even a tube of toothpaste. If you'll stop yapping and yacking and Yucatan ceases his ululations, we'll square away the yard and be off, Yokohama first stop. You all right Uriah? Yum-Yum? Yucatan? Then yoicks, yo-ho – and off we go!' That was last year; I fear the yawl is missing yet.

[k] and [g] are formed by raising the back of the tongue to meet the palate; this stops the air-flow; when the tongue is released a small explosion occurs: [k], and when voiced, [g]. Again, as with all the plosive consonants, care must be taken not to make the action so firm that a lot of air is pushing through during plosion. The jaw must be well released for these sounds and the resonance space behind the consonontal barrier kept open.

[k]

'Scudamore, can you cook?' asked the Duke. The Duke and his Cockney coachman were wrecked and castaway on a rocky outcrop in the Atlantic, when their ketch capsized in a squall, and in consequence the cuisine called for careful consideration. 'I've made a recce', continued the Duke, 'and come across capercaillie; there's skua, auk, cormorant, and skate I expect.' 'I can't be at your beck and call as cook, Duke, I'm coachman – could you catch us a donkey do you think?' He chuckled. 'It's equality now we're stuck on this murky kelp-cairn, Cock! If you want curried clams and auk you cook 'em.' The aristocrat scowled. 'It was a close call, Scudamore; if I'd not been capable of rescuing you you'd've been killed.' 'If your ketch hadn't leaked and caught her keel on that rock we wouldn't be wrecked. My contract doesn't call for castaway cooking.' 'An Eskimo'll come along in a kayak and rescue us I expect,' encouraged the Duke, 'now what about making a kitchen? – I'll catch you an auk.' Six weeks later, as forecast, the Eskimo came and found a couple of practically skeletal squabblers still squawking about kitchens and contracts.

[g]

Growing grapes in Glengiekie is a gleeless and grief-stricken business. Gloomily Guy McGraw got his gang together and gave them their grape-gathering gear. Glumly he glowered at the gaggle of rogues and vagabonds which had gorged on his eggs, glutted on his gruyère and gargled and glugged down his wine with gross and gargantuan greed to make ergs for the grape-picking. The ergs went in argument. The gang's gaudy garments would've gladdened any eye but McGraw's; that glaucous organ glistened with anxiety. It was time for the daily wrangle. The pickers grouped round Big Meg McGonagal, gorgon and guru, ogress eager for the hugger-mugger gripe and grab of 'negotiation'. Glossy with the grub he begrudged, she was engaged in guaging his strength with a termagant stare. 'The girls don't reckon that glutinous gruel you give us is good enough, gauleiter.' 'It's good.' 'It's goat.' 'It's goulash.' 'It's garbage.' 'Get gathering.' She guffawed, her dangling ear-rings and bangles jangling, and got to the point. 'The girls won't gather the grapes until you agree to give us no more goulash and another keg of rotgut.' 'OK, Bœuf Bourgignon it is, and two gallons of gamay.' 'Back to the grapes, girls,' growled Meg, vaguely aggrieved he'd given in so easily. McGraw gazed out at the glen with the ghost of a grin.

[h] is formed, usually, by simply allowing a clear passage for the airstream. The unresonated air which is passed through the mouth to form this sound should be kept to a practicable minimum, and little or none felt on a finger placed on the lips. It helps to think of the mouth/throat resonator being wide open and the [h] being formed at larynx level.

[h]

A   Help!
B   Who's that? Harry? How are you? Who're you howling at?
A   You, Horace; hurry, I'm hung up.
B   How horrible, Harry – does it hurt?
A   My haversack harness is half-hitched to the hayloft hoist and I'm being hauled higher and higher.

B   It looks quite hazardously hairy. Hang on and I'll hasten for help.

A   Horace you're a halfwit – you haven't the time. Do you hear?

B   How long before you hit your head on the hatch-beam?

A   Half an hour at most.

B   How do you halt the hoist?

A   How the hell should I know.

B   OK, hold on.

A   I *am* holding on, but the hoist is still heaving me heavenward and Hercules couldn't halt it just by hanging here.

B   I'll hop into Hayling and hurry along Henry Hollidge to help you.

A   How on earth shall I hang on for half an hour?

B   Hopefully, Harry, hopefully.

Vowels

[uː]

Who are you? Hubert? How do you do?

Do choose the cerulean blue shoes, Shula.

Don't toot your unmusical tuba in the Tube, Hugo, it's too much of a nuisance.

Loomis made oodles of boodle in Poona selling buhl pool tables.

[ʊ]

Prunella Hood, all woollens and worsteds, stood amid a roomful of books looking for 'Cooking from Uruguay to the Hindoo Kush' by Bulmer Bullen. It stood between 'Rookery Nook' and 'With Rucksack and Pushbike' by Hookham Crooke. She sat on a cushioned footstool and looked for a pudding: Butcher's Pudding with Worcester Sauce – she shook her head; Bulbul Pie – bulbul? Why? Woodcock and Mushroom Pudding with Zucchini and Couscous – she passed it by; then, A Pudding of Sugared Bullace! She decided to give it a good try.

[ɔː]

Don't maul the pawpaws, Paul.

Lord Borthwick called Lord Porthcawl a mawkish bore. It's

reported that this appalling performance by Borthwick has put Porthcawl off his port, and both authors are almost fraught at the thought that nothing short of war, tooth and claw, must now ensue.

[ɒ]

My odd long spotty socks got washed and the hot water's knocked their spots off. It's Oliver's fault, he washed them.

'The Cognac Trough' is a cod historical novel, waspishly snobbish, soft as a rotten squash, and constant only in the obstinate improbabilities of its plot.

[ɑː]

My father's a past master at driving a hard bargain but in a car he's a disaster.

Charlotte's from Arles, in France, and Ivana from Cardiff. Both are rather half-hearted about dancing in Dartmouth, in a melodrama called 'Marmaduke's a Martyr to Rhubarb', since they learned that after Dartmouth goes dark they go to Sark.

[ʌ]

The Puffing Gull has sunk in a sudden thunderstorm off Ushant.

Uncle Custance sups on mustard-smothered buckwheat and onions – that's for roughage; then curry, syllabub, honey-covered nuts, and a currant bun if he's still hungry; he shovels up all this stuff with gusto and then ends with a dozen or so cups of buttered rum.

[ɜː] and [ə]

Sir, your references to 'Bert the Burglar's Bird', considered by discerning experts my worthiest and most commercial work, are churlish and impertinent, and, furthermore, infernally hurtful. Yours etc., Ferdinand Turnip (Colonel, retd.).

The Earl's girlfriend's pearls weren't hers but the Earl's – but the furs were hers and she'd certainly earned them.

'It's about time I took out some insurance against the delivery of bad Cheddar and over-ripe Camembert', muttered the put-upon cheesemonger; 'I'm at the end of my tether and no mistake!'

[æ]

Alf's fashionable pal, Hal, lives off Pall Mall.

That hat's too flat, Pat.

The manager's banned that madman from the waxworks. He said the statues lacked contact with reality, and – can you imagine – the savage actually took the headsman's axe and began to bash and hack at them! He's done a fantastic amount of damage to Calamity Jane – her hat's round her ankles. Butch Cassidy's hands will have to be refashioned in new wax.

[e]

Good Heavens, jellied eggs for breakfast again!

Ellen, there's a fellow here says he's collecting for distressed gentlefolk. Can you spare tenpence, he says.

Seven zealous messengers from Edinburgh underwent many perilous adventures when they set off to deliver ten letters each to various addresses in the Hebrides. In relentlessly tempestuous weather, wet and unwell, they headed for their Hebridean destinations across the excessive swell of the deadly sea. Eventually the daring seven with their several letters met with success and delivered their messages: telephone bills.

[ɪ]

This is Sybil Smith who is sixth sibling of Wilfreda, Wilomena, Winifred, William and Winston. The six Smith children are sincerely sorry about appearing in so many silly tongue twisters and insist they are blameless in this.

William, called Billy, is a misogynist and a bit simple; rudely he calls his sister Wilomena, Willie Frilly Knickers and refuses to sit with her in the cinema. Winston sits and fishes and muses by various rivers and experiments in genetic engineering to make the fins of his tropical fishes more fancifully fringed.

Winifred is a singer and a bit unhinged.

[iː]

Wemyss is a wheeler-dealer in cheeses. His Brie is unbelievably evil. 'A steal at three pounds the kilo' says Wemyss.

Wheat and meat is all I eat; I'm neat of seat and fleet of feet.

Louise is the Bee Queen of Peebles because her teeth gleam and she seems sweet in a bikini; but she's no beekeeper that's easy to see. She screams if a bee breezes by her in the street.

Compound Vowels

[au]

How loud that cow sounds. It reminds me of Brown. Brown was louder.

All around town he pounded out the more astounding bits of Browning to dumbfounded crowds. Powerfully he drowned the shouts of the flower sellers round the fountain; cowled and gowned like a monk, he cowed or roused the crowds as he expounded in rounded vowels for hour after hour.

[uə]

Who're you?

Poor Stewart was so boorishly dour he could hardly endure the alluring and luxurious tourist guide Grua McLure. He abjured her rural moorland tours and took up painting murals which were curiously lurid. A casual reviewer called them 'The spuriously mercurial residue of an immature talent, injuriously fuelling an obscure inner fury. The jewelled fluorescence of The Wooer is perhaps truer to Stewart's nature.' 'Manure!' said Stewart.

[ai]

I fly my kite higher than Myra's.

Simon Mynott is a spy for Myerscough Diamond Mines. To keep prices high the diamond miners must limit supply. Sometimes private persons find riverine diamonds and try to get by the Mine's fixed prices by selling to private buyers. Enter Simon Mynott; likeable, naïve, a fine fellow – just the buyer the diamond finder sighs for. And cries about later – when he's violently deprived of his diamonds and finds he's in a bind with Myerscough Mines.

While filing piles of trial reports Miles smiles and smiles – why?

[əuͺ]

Oh go home Rowan.

I'm told these old moulds are for gold bowl-holders.
([oʊ] or [ɔʊ] is now widespread among Standard English speakers
before[ɫ].)

Don't go to Groves for your last loaf, Joan. Their loaves may be
whole-grain but they're so old they've grown wholly mouldy.

[eɪ]

Hey Wayne, today's the day of the game.

Patience Bleydell has an amazing way with clay. She shapes it into
apes, whales, snakes and sables. Layer by layer she agglomerates
the clay and, taking great pains and no haste, makes each graceful
detail. She animates the clay: the ape gazes half-afraid at the
strange snake, which, scaled in its delicately chased chain-mail
from head to tail, sways after its prey, a preening jay.

[ɛə]

Mary Kinnaird was scarcely prepared, when at the share-out of
Beyer Airways she found herself heiress. She had fair hair, cut
square, and a daring, care-free air; but once in an aeroplane she
was scared when a garish scarecrow of a man sat in the chair
beside her and began to stare. Mary found it almost unbearable;
and when he produced a questionnaire and asked her to share
her thoughts on hare coursing, dairy farming, air fares, and how
Aquarians compared to Arians, she was wary as well as scared.
But the scarecrow had been Airey Beyer the aircraft manufacturer
– and now she was his heiress. He must've been rarely impressed.

[ɪə]

We're really here, dear.

Piers Speering, bearded, bleary and queerly dressed in mysterious
Indian regalia, steered clear of any serious career. They offered
to serialize his weird adventures in India as 'The Eerie Series'. He
cleared the tears from his eyes, rubbed his ear and said 'Cheers
dears – but no fear! Seriously, it could interfere with the salubrious
and superior experience of drinking beer.'

[ɔɪ]

Avoid lawyers and rejoice!

Boyle is a boisterous roisterer, noisy of voice and void of vice. His choicer exploits such as poisoning his lawyer's oysters, or annoying his hoity-toity and exploitative employer by soiling his corduroys with an oily moisturizer, are done for enjoyment. He's a right royal trencherman too. I once watched him hoist a whole joint of broiled loin of pork with oyster sauce and coils of boiled noodles.

Speech faults

All speech faults can be summed up in one generality: they impede the wished-for communication by drawing our attention to the speech process rather than to that which we wish to communicate. Let's consider some of those which are fairly typical and often met with.

1   Sounds which are malformed because of the dysfunction of part or whole of the speech mechanism. Such would be stuttering; the effect upon speech of a cleft palate; a lisp; the poor sounding of [ɹ] and [l] because the tongue-string is too short; the effects of a stroke which has resulted in the partial paralysis of the speech organs. It is not my intention to try to deal with these sorts of problem here; they can be more effectively treated by a speech therapist. (Although it is worth noting that some stutterers find they can obtain a remission of their speech problem by practising stopping the habitual response, freeing the neck, and working to produce a good fullness of resonance; also, the lisp may occur where there is no damage to the speech organs and no basic abnormality and in this case can be treated as would be the speech faults in the second group.)

2   Sounds which are badly produced because the organs of articulation, though uninjured and capable of correct functioning, are not in fact making the right speech-shapes. Some speakers, for example, allow a spill of air across the sides of the tongue when pronouncing [s] and so end up saying a sound which is a mixture

of [s] and [l] and [ʃ]. Such abnormalities can be corrected, and usually fairly easily, by stopping the habitual pattern and taking thought as to how the sound should be and how it is made; part of the process will involve sensitizing the organs of articulation responsible for making the sound, and this is best done by moving them into and out of the required shapes silently so that sound does not detract from sensation; then breath is passed through the speech-shape as it is formed, and finally voice is added. However, speech correction is a laborious business and you will find it easier to work on this kind of fault with a good speech teacher rather than to go it alone.

3 Sounds which are malformed because the relationship between the action of the breath and that of the organs of articulation is faulty. This covers a wide range and most of this section of the book has concerned itself with the efficient functioning of this relationship.

4 Sounds which are properly formed but are too attention-catching. An example might be the intrusion of a foreign or regional accent; the sounds may be well formed in themselves, but they catch the attention too much because – in the context – they are the wrong sounds, or at least not those which are expected. Another example might occur when the speech sounds are properly made, but the hearer is aware that the speaker has to make an unusual effort to say them, or perhaps is over-precise in his speech – this often leads to an uneasy use of speech rhythms and it's this which betrays the effort being made by the speaker.

5 Speech mannerisms, such as a tendency to dwell over-long on one sound or not to pronounce a sound when it should be pronounced; or perhaps the mannerism might be a characteristic but unusual inflectual pattern. Such tics are usually taken care of by thinking and using the Stop–Release process – conscious control in other words.

With particular speech faults correction is usually a lengthy business, particularly if you are working by yourself. The corrective hints with the foregoing practice paragraphs should be some help, but usually the process can be speeded up with the help of an

experienced teacher who knows the short-cuts to solving your
particular problem.

For a fuller description of the speech sounds I recommend A. C.
Gimson's *An Introduction to the Pronunciation of English* (Arnold).

Intention

We have examined some of the things which are likely to go wrong
with voice and speech, and underlying the work so far has been an
assumption of an ideal quality of sound. But ideal for what? Ideal
for filling a large space with clearly audible speech, yes, but that is
only a start and so far we have more or less confined ourselves to
the mechanics of the business; but speech is for communication,
which is a process of response to changing needs. Subject to
the governing objective of wanting to share something with the
audience, our immediate intention may change from moment to
moment: now the audience is responsive, now it isn't; suddenly
there is a heckler; because of *this* moment, *this* word or phrase has
a heightened importance and these phrases and words are less
important. Then for the actor there may be the demands of
characterization; perhaps the character is a coughing, introverted
consumptive, or someone with a marked speech defect, or a voice
which sounds like a gargle, or the spit and hiss of a snake.

It really doesn't matter *what* demands are made by the need to
characterize, by the situation, by the temper of the audience or the
whim of the actor – all the usages of voice production and speech
are capable of modification according to the needs of the moment;
but the principles of efficient breath control, economical tuning and
clear speech remain, and it is for the actor to decide how he can
best apply those principles in the given situation. If he has the
fundamental principles at work in his normal voice and speech, is
accustomed to a mechanically efficient use and understands how it
works, he should experience little difficulty in arriving at a *practical*
modification of his use in the acting situation, because he will have
the control which confers the freedom to change.

In the end, the speaker's success or failure is measured by the
response of his audience. Since this is so, it makes for a certain
difficulty during practice time. At home we may practise the

mechanics of our voice and speech, work on our use and perfect our breathing, but the moment we go before an audience we are likely to forget all these mechanical considerations because we are so overcome by the pressing need to communicate, which is our prime function. Notwithstanding the probability that we should actually communicate better in such a moment were we to be free enough to use the *means whereby* which we have been working to acquire, we throw ourselves, as it were, into the gaining of the end and let the means go hang. In such a moment you may feel that a good deal of your preparation has been irrelevant. Where before you worked on your breathing to satisfy yourself or to perfect the controlling of it, as if it were an end in itself, now you find that the act of breathing itself has a communicative importance, and suddenly you want to do it all differently; the well-modulated pitch of the voice which you cherished at home goes by the board as you sense that it leaves the audience cold. This is the moment of truth and you find yourself unprepared; your reaction is likely to be a kind of panic.

So can you prepare for that moment? Not entirely, no; because the audience is always different. Experience will teach you a lot, and after a few performances you will begin to read your audiences more effectively and to know what sort of changes are *likely* to occur in your work the moment you take it to the public. However, there is some preparation you can make against that moment of truth. The first is to choose and prepare pieces – poems, stories, anecdotes, jokes, songs, speeches from plays – and try them out on people. Actors have an advantage over other public speakers here, for it is a necessary part of the actor's life to work on his skills each day and so it is usually not difficult for him to find a like-minded actor with whom a critical exchange can be made. Also he has rehearsal time – particularly valuable if he can use the rest of the cast as an audience. A third and important point is this: if you have no captive friend to use as an audience when you practise, at least imagine an audience; or, to put it another way, don't let your practice become introverted; use the furniture as your audience; give yourself an *outward* focus. This applies even if you are playing an introverted character in the most private of situations; in the end, his introversion and privacy have to be made so public that they fill the theatre and hold the audience. So whatever other intentions you may have, one which goes along with all the rest, and justifies them in the theatre, is the intention to communicate.

Choose your pieces for practice with all of your needs as an actor in mind, not just to improve your articulation or your breathing or to help you exercise a weak area in your resonation – although these are laudable-enough objectives. Keep the larger view. An actor is a professional changer and what he changes is the way he uses and projects himself. However, at war against an ideal state of freedom to choose how we shall use ourselves and embody our intentions, are our various predelictions and aversions; it is as if we are prepared to use parts of our make-up and not others, and nowhere is this seen more strongly than in the attitudes and emotions which we choose to exploit, or reject, as actors. If you are to avoid the unbalancing effects of your predelictions and aversions, you ought to get to know what they are. Those areas in your make-up which you shy away from using are probably the areas you need to find a way of using; it may mean digging around inside yourself to find a way of using a relatively dormant source of motivation, but it's worth it in the end, and necessary if you are to be, in fact, an adequate professional changer.

Your practice material, by the time you have been working for a few months, will be extensive and varied – the more varied the better; but don't let this tempt you to imitate the action of the butterfly; work consistently with a piece until you feel you have solved the problem it set you.

Speech and characterization

Speech is often not exploited enough in the theatre as a means of characterization. The use of regional accent is of course well enough established to need no comment here; but there are many things which the speech pattern can convey to a reasonably informed ear apart from the geographical provenance of a character. For example, different generations have their particular uses in pronunciation and vocabulary, although the choice of the latter is usually left to the writer in the theatre. Different social strata have different speech uses, and – a point which is often overlooked – families develop idiosyncratic uses of tune, rhythm and phrasing, and pronunciation, and often of voice production as well. The actor should analyse, perhaps with the help of his friends, what information his own speech pattern conveys so that he may be aware of his own idiosyncrasies and not foist them on a character for whom they are quite unsuitable.

Also, as part of his preparation for a role, he should undertake the research which might be necessary for him to convey an accurate impression of the full background of his character through his speech. I remember attending a performance of Brecht's *Caucasian Chalk Circle* where great care had been taken over the theatrical uses of speech. The central character, Grusha Vashnadze, undertakes a long journey in the course of which she suffers various adventures; the sense of the journey was conveyed very well in the changes of accent employed by the actors playing the characters she encountered along the road; then, too, the various social groups were well defined in speech terms: the aristocrats, while preserving individuality as characters, were able to suggest a homogeneity of background by taking some voice and speech characteristics in common. The end result was a clear definition of the characters and also of a complete social and geographical background. Properly researched, and worked, the speech pattern itself will communicate as much about a character as his actions and words.

Whisper and stage whisper

In a true whisper, as we have seen, all of the speech sounds are produced entirely without voice. On the stage, if the theatre is small, and if the space has good acoustic properties, there is no reason why a true whisper should not be used. But usually, in order to get the sound of the whisper to reach all parts of the theatre, the actor has to pump out air at a prodigal rate and finds in consequence that he has great difficulty in getting out more than half-a-dozen words on a breath. Perhaps because of this, the convention of the 'stage whisper' came into being. All that distinguishes it from the true whisper is that a very little amount of voice is introduced and so what you end up with is extremely breathy voice production; however, it is more economical of breath than the true whisper. The stage whisper depends for its clarity on the very sharp and precise definition of the consonants; because there is more breath than voice carrying these, you will find that the articulatory movements need to be firmer, on the whole, than for normal voice production. However, don't overdo this firming up and pay particular attention to freedom of jaw movement. Performed in this way, the stage whisper can be a useful articulation exercise, and will certainly test the precision with which you form the consonants.

USING YOUR VOICE

Playing with the voice

Don't be afraid to play with the voice. Step outside the narrow tracks of your ordinary voice use as a regular part of your training. Until you have experimented a lot you don't know the capabilities of your voice. You can risk sounding like an idiot if you are practising privately, and, unless you have a job on hand, you can even risk a little strain in the cause of finding out. In any case, if you keep your basic good use you won't hurt yourself beyond quick repair. If you find something hurts or tires you too quickly, you should have the tools of analysis to find out how and why you went wrong and you can make the necessary corrections the next time.

Exercises for playing with the voice

Here are some suggestions:

1 Read aloud and perfect the characterization of children's stories; particularly those with a lot of different characters speaking – the more fantastic the better.

2 The same thing with comics. Here you have pictures to work from, and the pictures give you the characterization. First try, however inadequately nature may have constructed you for the task, to empathize physically with the character as the cartoonist has drawn him. Try to achieve the physical rhythm of the creature, as suggested by the pictures; from this begin to play with the resonance and pitch of the voice until you have achieved a clear differentiation between the various characters. Think, even in the

most absurd and far-fetched cases, what the impulsive force is that makes the creature speak: in other words, motivate the script.

3 Coming slightly nearer to the adult world, try finding the vocal noise which makes advertisements work. In this, look particularly for the attitude behind the script. It will imply a relationship with the audience and with the product you are trying to sell. Some advertisements have a compression of language and an exactness of intention that makes them the poems of the world of commerce. In a skilfully written advertisement each word will be important. Realizing the intention which lies behind the choice of each word is very taxing and often calls for great control of the nuances of tone, inflexion, and so on.

4 Recitals: put together a performance of your favourite writing, prose and poetry. Choose your material first because you like it and think an audience might too, and then, for your own instruction and amusement, make sure it offers you virtuoso scope for your voice.

5 Singing: sing as much as you can. This exercises your control of pitch and time. The usefulness of singing is that it is 'tuned, *sustained*, speech'.* You can examine the processes almost at leisure while you sing a slow song. In any event, actors today need to be able to sing with reasonable efficiency, so you might as well get in some practice! And while you are singing, move. You don't have to do an energetic dance, but move to make sure you aren't 'holding on'.

For further suggestions see Voice and Movement below.

Voice and movement

Voice, when it is used communicatively, is an extension of gesture. It is a process of movement in itself.

In communicative speech the speaker is always trying to reach

*W. Shakespeare, *Plain Words on Singing* (Putnam).

someone else. A journey is implied. At its most urgent it's as if we want to jump inside the skin of the person we are talking to, to say 'This is me, this is what my meaning feels like'. Or sometimes it's as if we are inviting the listener to make the journey to inhabit us. When there is something really important to be said it always has a gestural root and shares the communicative and emotional impulse with the whole of our person. An actor, whatever character he is playing and regardless of the situation the character is in, when he speaks is always saying something of importance to him because he always has the very strong motivation of reaching and involving his audience.

This is why although in some situations the actor is required to use his voice interpretively while remaining fairly still (on radio and in the dubbing studio for example) nevertheless he must not allow that to inhibit him physically to the point where the body/voice relationship suffers. Such an inhibition has a deadening or falsifying effect on the voice. It can seem as if there is a divorce between the voice and the emotional, and basically physical, impulses which are the motivation to speak; then the performance sounds over-intellectual, or as if the speaker is guarded and resistant to the communicative impulse. Some public speakers, of course, are at pains to present themselves in just such a way: 'Emotion has not influenced my judgement here; reason rules my life'. More normally our problem with communication is to share ourselves, not to hide. But the actor's use of the alliance between voice and movement does not mean that he has to live entirely off his passions. It's the balance between the emotional and the rational which he seeks and the freedom to allow responsive changes in that balance. The body and voice must be free to express this, as well as experience it.

A famous Russian director once said that he should be able to place a perspex wall between his actors and the audience and the audience should still be able to tell what was going on, what relationships and characters were on stage, merely by seeing them.

In a way that makes sense. The basic pattern of body use conveys the relationship of the person with self and with others. The local and temporary changes within that basic use from moment to moment convey the shifting nuances and importances within those relationships and within the acts of communication which are taking place. As these changes take place, normally the voice changes as well – it follows the body, as it were. This being so, when you deliberately choose for characterization purposes to change the basic pattern of use, you don't need to work out the fundamental voice change. It's latent in the overall body change and will emerge given the time to allow this.

It is possible to work the other way on as well, and a lot of actors do. They find the voice of the character and let the body change accordingly. Since the two are inextricably bound together it shouldn't matter which way one works; the basic idea is the same: to kick the imagination to work, through the whole person, towards the fullest possible realization of another state of being; however, most actors in fact find it easier to allow their imaginations to work on the body and through that to the voice.

Laban

If you radically change your body use, you change your relationship with yourself and the world around you. Rudolph Laban made an effective and important study of types of movement which explores these relationships and it's most useful to the actor. It reveals, above all, the areas of self which we customarily ignore – emotional and relational states of being which we normally prefer not to explore. For the actor who wishes not to be forever bound within the confines of his behavioural predilictions, a study of Laban's work and the practice of some of the basic changes of body states he describes must inevitably lead to a growth in awareness of the actor's clichés and of the enormous possibilities of development open to him in escaping them. This will show in the voice. Once you have lived long enough within the change of movement dynamic, or 'effort', for it to have begun to work on your imagination, it will affect your pitch use, resonation, the whole rhythm of your breathing – and hence your speech rhythm – the pace and the inflexion pattern of your voice. This is an organic and unintellectual way of approaching voice development for acting. Although detailed analysis is called for at the start when studying any basic body change, once you have begun to live it in extended improvisation, synthesis of the disparate elements happens almost automatically and you find you are, for the moment, *living* differently. The body feeds you the information and your actor's sensibility and imagination, if you go with it, will do the rest.

Weight change

Try this exercise and see what happens to your voice.

1 Imagine yourself to be very light. Walk and move until this lightness is working right through you.

2 Speed up your movement till it is what you would consider fast (in relation to your own normal speed).

3 Keeping this body state, begin to talk – give a description of what you're doing, anything which fits the state you find yourself in.

This process, particularly 1 and 2, should be given a good deal of time; it's not so much the mechanical change in itself which is important, but what happens as your imagination gets to work; see where it takes you, what sort of behaviour emerges as appropriate to this body state. Let the improvisation range over a number of familiar activities and see how they change in consequence of your continued lightness. Finally let it work through into voice. When you've spent an hour or so being light and fast, try changing the dynamic to slow and heavy. There are vast numbers of possible permutations of just these two elements alone (speed and weight); there are other elements to be considered as well. I list the titles of helpful guides in the Bibliography. They will take you much further in terms of movement changes.

Animals

Actors use many techniques to escape from the everyday self and kick their imaginations into the creative state which lets them find the character they need to play. Dirk Bogarde has said he finds his characters partly by finding the right shoes to wear. Several actors have used this technique. A change of use that begins with the feet can affect the whole psychosomatic balance if you allow the imagination to work with it.

One way to change your everyday self and at the same time reveal a lot about the selves you don't normally become, is the study of animals. Animal work has formed part of the training of actors in drama schools for a long time, and richly rewarding it can be.

The method of work in this context is less that of direct imitation than the use of your empathetic ability. As you watch the animal, you are imagining yourself to be the animal, feeling responses in your own body to the way the animal moves and sounds. In the studio you might start by trying to reproduce the animal's movements as nearly as possible; but that is only to check the accuracy of your observation. The next stage is to allow the essence of the animal, as you perceive it and empathize with it, to take over and move you, and make noise through you. Imaginatively you are at one with the animal. This will provoke in you an awareness of another kind of relationship with yourself and your surroundings. As your awareness of the change increases, go with it, see where it takes you. Eventually a synthesis of behaviour and relationships will emerge which is different from your own and amounts to a character. Eventually, too, the animal, which was only the starting point for this change, will cease to be important – except perhaps as a point of reference – and your behaviour, though changed, will be completely humanized. In any case, your observation of the animal is not zoological but anthropocentric – it's another form of you you are looking for and find.

The postural fix and predetermined interpretation

The gallery of 'characters' which emerge from working through Laban's dynamic efforts show the actor to himself in a richness of behavioural patterns sufficient to make sense of all the broad and simplified characters of the medieval Mystery plays – and a good few more besides; but in themselves they don't add up to fully rounded characters in the psychological sense. What they provide is a kinaesthetic basis of change; a matrix which adapts as you begin to sense a gamut of behaviour which more or less fits with the personality suggested by it. The point is that the change of use of the body does suggest a whole series of inner changes. All the changes taken together cohere in a pattern of behaviour and response, and when that point of cohesion is reached by the actor it's as if he had discovered a different personality. He hasn't become a different person, because his experiences, tastes and beliefs are still his – only, for a while, in abeyance, as he chooses to explore another synthesis of some of the elements of self. It is an act of physical imagination. It's made possible by allowing it to happen and having a physical sensibility well enough equipped, and free enough, to carry the permission through into action.

A great deal of characterization in the theatre falls far short of the kind of change and quality of exploration I've described above; often because it's not necessary – the role lies close to the actor – more often because it takes more time than rehearsal allows; most often perhaps because even when actors feel the part they are playing calls for radical change, the changes they in fact make are fairly superficial because the basis of personal physical use is still that of habit. I suspect this is partly why when casting a play and riffling through the pages of *Spotlight* one ends up with some kind of type-casting. Not necessarily the casting to physical or vocal type – though that happens with great frequency – but casting according to the type of performance one envisages the actor giving. You've seen some of the actor's work and from that, in your mind's eye, you arrive at a type of performance by that actor, no matter what the role.

Often, happily, one is wrong in one's assumptions; and there are a few actors of such versatility that you cannot with any certainty imagine their performance in role x or y. But in a large number of cases, the performance you have imagined the actor giving is roughly the performance he does give. I suspect what the mind's eye is looking at when it contains an image of the performance the actor has not yet given is the clichés of physical use and reaction, the fixed patterns of response to the act of acting which belong to that actor. The chances are the actor himself is not altogether aware of them; an exception would have to be made in the case of any actor who has made, and perhaps carefully nursed, a reputation founded on his ability to play one character superbly well; he probably knows exactly what he's doing and has chosen to do it. But most actors don't choose to limit themselves; most actors feel within them the possibilities of an infinite variety of behaviour. They are not fooling themselves in that; only sometimes deluding themselves in thinking that's what they're achieving. Within a fixed range of postural behaviour, the interpretation of the role also finds its limits. Fine if the role fits the actor's fixed range, but what if it doesn't? Well, it's part of the actor's job as a professional changer to be able to unfix his range and make the necessary journey towards the role. The work suggested in the first part of this book, and the Laban work, should together offer a means whereby the actor can unfix his limits.

Empathy and imitation

Empathy is the state which exists when imaginatively you identify with the subject of your study; it produces a shift of outlook and a physical change. It's one of the most formidably useful ways the actor can employ his imagination, and leads to the deepest understanding of what people are and how they function of which we are capable. The actor who has successfully empathized with someone may not be able to describe his understanding in words, but this hardly matters – the proper and effective mode through which the actor shows this understanding is behaviour.

The most obvious use of empathy for the actor occurs when he wishes to represent some non-fictional person. If his subject is living and if he can work with him directly so much the better. But filmed record is good to work from – often easier than working face to face with the subject since you can run through film as many times as you wish. If film and the subject himself are not available then any voice recording is a good starting point; to some extent even photographs may serve if there are enough of them. The interesting thing about the process of empathy, as distinct from mimicry, is that although you are working initially from your perception of externals, of how the body moves, how the voice sounds and so on, the straight imitation of these externals is only a means to achieving some interior knowledge of who the subject is; you have to feel at the end of the process that you know how to behave as the subject in all circumstances. This may not *be* so; but the character must *feel* that complete to you. It is the wholeness of your realization which convinces the audience. By the time you come to play the role you may have modified some of the externals in a way the mimic is not at liberty to do; he has to stick with them and get them as exactly right as possible.

Setting out to copy someone's accent or voice use, you will probably go through a phase of conscious analysis as you try to understand what you have to do to produce your voice and speech in the same way; but it is the less consciously analytical process of empathizing with the subject which will bring you, in the end, to talk with the necessary freedom and fluency of a real life being lived, and by this stage you're not really copying the subject at all. You've liberated into action the you which stands for the subject.

What holds good as a process for representing a real person to some extent works as well when you are playing a fictional role. You start with the given data – the character says and does these things; your job is then to make living sense of the data until everything is absorbed into a pattern of living which could extend outside the confines of the play. You evolve a series of images of the character and you move towards inhabiting them until they come to life for you. You are empathizing with these images, much as you might with a filmed representation of a person. As you empathize with these images – or imagine yourself as that person – they teach you their fuller meaning and make increasing demands upon your body and voice by way of change, until there is no longer an image, only you behaving, and feeling, and using your voice differently.

Working on accents

Usually the working up of a regional or foreign accent takes a long time, unless you're a gifted mimic, and so you can expect to have to do most of the work either before rehearsals begin or in your free time at home during rehearsals.

The ideal thing to do when you're working on the accent is to go to the place where it's in normal everyday use and work on it there. However, this is not practicable in most situations so the usual way is to work from tape recordings. You must make sure you have an adequate supply for the accent under consideration. There are various commercial recordings available, but you will probably find they are not adequate and you will need to supplement them with material of your own. In any event, it's a good idea always to have available a collection of tapes of the more usual British and American regional accents. If you are making your own tapes, the way you go about it needs consideration.

The sample tape recording

First you must find native speakers of the accent; recording actors who have studied the accent is very much second best. You should try to record more than one person so that you can determine what are merely the subjects' idiosyncrasies and which speech elements they have in common. Try to get specimens of conversation which cover the whole normal range of speech use, including questions, statements, exclamations and shifts of mood and changes of intention. Recording a subject reading may, if you choose your text carefully, give you a comprehensive sample of all the speech sounds, but it will have reading rhythms and inflexions and will probably be far from conversational. You may do well to start with such a piece of text and then fill the rest of the tape with chat or an interview. (The Practice Paragraphs in the section on Speech contain between them pretty well all the basic conjunctions of sound and may be useful for recording purposes; each consonant is joined to as many different vowels as possible, so recording a couple of the consonant paragraphs could be a great help. Also, if there is a particular sound in the accent you feel you might need to concentrate on, again, the Practice Paragraph will be useful.) Quite often people react to the presence of a microphone by slowing down their speech and being over-careful. This will distort the natural rhythm and tune, so make sure your subject is in a fairly relaxed frame of mind before you start – a couple of drinks may help. Alternatively you could try recording the chat part of the sample without letting the subject know he is being recorded – but don't forget to get his permission to use it afterwards.

Having secured your tape recording you can press on with learning the accent. There are different ways of going about this and experience will show you which is best for you. The first is a less consciously analytical approach to processing the information. Leave the tape running for as long and as often as you can and allow the sounds to sink in while you are doing something else. Gradually, as you become familiar with the tape, you can talk along with it, following the rhythm and tune and allowing the accent to drift into your own speech. Don't try to work hard at this. Play the tape and speak with it while you're cooking or cleaning or going for a walk. Then leave the tape running in the background and talk back to it, using the accent; argue with it, question it; make a dialogue. Gradually you will feel that you can carry on talking in the accent without needing the constant reminder of the tape. Now you should record yourself and match the results against the sample. If all seems well, try a conversation with someone and record that. If you notice there are sounds for which your version of the accent sounds consistently wrong, you will probably have to examine the making of the sounds in question. This is a consciously analytical way of doing things which can be used for understanding the whole of the speech pattern; it's more tedious, but thorough.

Accent analysis

You will need a check-list of the vowels and consonants and two tape recorders. What you are going to attempt to do is find out what substitutions are made in the accent you are learning for the sounds in your check-list. This approach is made easier if you have some knowledge of phonetics and certainly you will need to make some kind of phonetic transcription as you go. The phonetic symbols for Standard English are listed in the section on Speech pp. 133–8.

Take one sound at a time, beginning with the vowels; play the tape through until you've got a clear feeling of the difference between your sound (or the Standard English sound) and the accent sample. Try to feel what your tongue and lips have to do to make the accent sound. You may find that there is a straight substitution of one vowel for another: [aɪ] becomes [ɔɪ] or [ɑ:] becomes [æ]. Often, things are complicated by the kind of resonance used – the tongue/lip-shape might be [ɑ:], but the vowel is nasalized. All this you note. Then you try saying the substitution, with the appropriate Practice Paragraph, until you're sure of the new sound.

Now try saying a phrase or sentence in imitation of the sample. Record it on your second recorder and play the original and then your version to see how they compare. As you analyse more sounds, the phrase you are imitating will sound more and more like the original. At the same time, because you are playing key phrases over and over, their tune and inflexion pattern will gradually sink in and you should find, by the end of your vowel substitution analysis, that the rhythm and tune of the original has been absorbed. The key phrases will be useful later to get you going as you begin to apply the accent to the part: merely saying one or two key phrases should bring the whole accent back into focus.

After you've worked on the vowels, you should be aware if there are consonants which are different or not used. If you're not sure, go on with the analysis until you are, working at the consonants just as you did the vowels.

The point about working this way is that, in the end, you should have acquired a good knowledge of how the accent is put together and be able to improvise in it with a reasonable chance of success. This is unlikely to happen with the third way of working.

Recording the role

This method requires you to work, from the beginning, with the script. You obtain a recording of your part in the required accent. You listen to it phrase by phrase and imitate it, making recordings on your second recorder to compare imitation and original. This method is often used in films and television by actors who have a crowded schedule; it doesn't usually lead to a mastery of the accent, only to the ability to use it for the script. I find this way of working a bit sterile and unduly limiting because you are more or less committed to saying the line in one way. If you change the motivation and action of the line, you may find you no longer know how to say it and maintain the accent.

You might have some difficulty getting the kind of recording you want for this way of working. The reading you work from should be as near to your interpretation of the part as possible and this might mean you find yourself giving the reader impromptu acting lessons. This is one case, therefore, where it is probably better to consult a professional accent teacher and get her or him to make the tape for you.

Rehearsal for the theatre

Properly used, rehearsal time exercises just about all of the actors' skills, and a detailed discussion of how to make the most of rehearsal would need a book to itself. Here we are concentrating on the uses of voice and speech, but because these are only elements in a complex of many activities which constantly interact, we must necessarily consider how some of these interactions are likely to affect voice and speech.

Home preparation

At home is where you absorb the information and practise the skills which you will not have time to worry about when you are working with the other actors. In the rehearsal room your attention will be more on what you are doing than how you do it – the action/reaction of line and scene. If the role calls for a change of speech use – a regional accent or a stammer, say – then this has to be worked up at home so that you can begin to act with it when you get to the rehearsal room. The same would apply to a voice use which requires a lot of practice; if you find that your role demands a particular pitch range or resonance, home is the place to work out *how* you do it. Some of this preparation may perhaps begin before the first rehearsal, particularly if you have the script in advance and the director has given you some background information to work up and research. During the scramble of rehearsal there is seldom much time for the actor to undertake serious research on the background to his role so he must do that in his own time.

Two practical examples: in *Body and Soul* by Roy Kendall a priest undergoes a sex-change operation and, when the play opens, has been receiving hormone treatment for about a year; this has produced various physical effects including some voice change. If the part is played by an actress, she probably has to concentrate on working the lower range of the voice, while bearing in mind that the voice is unsettled and in a state of change. To find out what happens to a man's voice during such treatment, the actress will need to find recordings of those who have undergone it and study them. She may need to consult doctors and, if possible, contact someone who has had the operation and discuss its effects (she would want to do this for the sake of the characterization as well as to study the vocal effects). Hormone treatment of the kind described in the play tends to affect the cords in such a way that for a certain time the pitch-break occurs. Learning to use the pitch-break will take a great deal of practice and the foundations for its use must be laid during home preparation.

A second example would be the character of Matieu in Feydeau's *L'Hôtel du Libre Échange* (variously translated as *Hotel Paradiso* and *A Little Hotel on the Side*). Matieu is a stammerer – a rather odd stammerer since he only stammers when it's raining. There are several kinds of stammer and not all of them are likely to be appropriate to the part and workable in terms of the farce; and the stammer needs to be convincingly done. If the actor playing Matieu has never been a stammerer he will need to research the part; he needs to know how to stammer, what kind of stammer to choose, what behaviour patterns may go with the stammer and so on. Finding out all of this information may entail a visit to a speech clinic and some hours spent observing stammerers, perhaps talking to them and recording them; and if he still doesn't have the information he wants, perhaps he'll need to read a book about stammering.

These fairly extreme changes in voice and speech use come from facts known about the characters right from the beginning and so can be worked on at home. Most changes in voice and speech, however, would emerge as the process of characterization develops and we'll come to that later.

Rehearsal warm-up

Give yourself a warm-up before beginning rehearsal. Sometimes this is done as a company activity, but more often than not there isn't time, and if different actors are called at different times to rehearse their various scenes it's impracticable to hold company warm-ups until the run-through stage of rehearsal is reached, when the whole company will be on call. If you're not physically, vocally and imaginatively prepared for rehearsal you will find it takes you longer to get going and valuable rehearsal time is lost. (See An Actor's Warm-Up.)

The reading

The first rehearsal is usually given over to a straight read-through of the play at which some actors will attempt to give a suggestion of character – if characterization is called for – and others will content themselves with the simplest kind of rendering leaving the character to emerge through rehearsal. The reading will probably lead into a fairly lengthy discussion of the play, the characters and their interrelationships. It may be the last time until the run-through when the whole company is together. So this is a good time to settle company policy in various matters some of which may be to do with voice and speech. If you are going to need time outside of director's rehearsals to work with the other actors to establish a family speech use or a shared regional accent, now is when you need to make the point so that rehearsal schedules can be contrived with this in mind. A play which poses a large number of policy decisions with regard to speech and voice use is *Life's A Dream* by Calderón de la Barca, so it's a good practical example to consider.

The heroine of the piece, Rosaura, together with her servant Clarín, comes to Poland from the Dukedom of Muscovy. In the beginning she is disguised as a young man. This disguise is maintained until later in the play she confesses to Clotaldo that she is a woman. At a naturalistic level, therefore, this part poses two questions, one of voice use and one of speech use: should the actress playing Rosaura disguise her voice to sound more like a man? And should she and Clarín – and the Muscovite Prince Astolfo, who also comes to the Polish court – have a speech pattern which is different from that of the Polish courtiers? These questions lead us towards a definition of the fundamental concept of the play, so they need to be answered at this stage rather than later.

The director may decide that since the play is not naturalistic it is sufficient that the characters say they come from Muscovy, that they don't need to make a point of being foreign in speech. Conversely, particularly if the notion of who wears the Polish crown is seen as an issue in the play, and that an important part of the action is the refusal of the Polish soldiers and peasantry to accept a Muscovite usurper as heir to the Polish crown, perhaps a marked speech contrast between Poles and Muscovites will be called for. In this case, are the actors playing Muscovites to use a Russian accent? Or an invented one? The text is written with great intricacy of rhyme and metre in the Spanish original and some current translations have followed suit, so any change of speech would have to ensure that the verse structure is not needlessly sacrificed to the accent – so, exactly what and how much speech change should be made? Then, too, if accents are to be used, should the social differences between Clarín and his Muscovite superiors Rosaura and Astolfo be indicated? Because Clarín is a servant does he necessarily speak worse 'Polish'? And, in the scenes between Rosaura and Clarín or Rosaura and Astolfo is the accent dropped on the assumption that they are no longer talking 'Polish'?

Then there is the question of voice in the character of Rosaura. This may not arise if the actress playing the part has a voice of the type which anyway sounds sexually ambivalent. However, let's suppose that her voice normally sounds feminine. What kind of voice change is she going to have to make? Does the 'young man' have to sound like a young man or is it sufficient to rely on costume and the behavioural changes which that makes to establish masculinity? During the action of the play Rosaura encounters Segismundo who has been kept a prisoner since infancy and has never met a woman. The sound of Rosaura's voice has a profound effect on Segismundo – why? Because it is a woman's voice, or because of the kind of person she is? Meeting the chained Segismundo produces a state of shock in Rosaura – does she forget to speak with her man's voice when she meets him? And then remember to use it again later in the same scene when she is confronted by Clotaldo – who seems thoroughly taken in by her disguise until she reveals the truth?

One could play around with various permutations of behaviour in considering the use of accent and voice for the role of Rosaura, but properly, the questions I have suggested would, if asked, be quickly and easily answered at the reading because the answers will be supplied by the director's concept of the essential action of the play. However, these are the kinds of questions which the actors will be asking *themselves* at the reading and they need a public airing so that everyone is quite clear about what they are to do.

On the floor

There are as many ways of developing the rehearsal after the reading as there are directors; some directors, traffic directors one might call them, go straight to blocking the moves for the play, sometimes with and sometimes without consulting the actors; they tend to be more concerned with visual aspects of the show than with the meaning of the text, and leave the actors to work out meaning, character and relationships by themselves. Other directors will spend considerable time with the actors working out background and relationships, improvising where necessary, and so move gradually towards a definition of the action. They will find the moves which satisfy the needs of the actors in realizing their relationships, so that the actors' personal sense of the character's action develops alongside the intrinsic movement of the play into an organically evolved whole. But whatever kind of director you are working with, at some point during rehearsal, actors and director have to agree about what the action is: what are the characters doing? Why? When? Who are they? And in the end the action will be the sum of answers to these and other such questions. Each different character provokes its own specific questions: what physical state is the character in? How old? Doing what kind of work? What are the loves, hates and interests of the character? How was the character educated? What is the character's framework of references and background? And many more questions. This is where the role gains definition as the answers provoke change.

Rehearsal is partly a journey from this consciously speculative state of asking the questions to the state where the answers have been found and the results absorbed so that the actor is at ease with them to the point where they seem his natural and comfortable behaviour in the world of the play. The half-way stage on this journey is where most problems arise. Knowledge about the role which has come to the actor quite consciously needs translating into muscular, emotional and mental responses which are no longer being worked out in the front of the brain. This is 'getting the feel of the part'.

Going towards the role: blocks

Put at its simplest, there are two ways of arriving at the definition of the role: either the actor changes himself to play it, or he adapts the role and plays it from within his customary range; usually he does a bit of both. Moving towards the role takes the actor into areas of great uncertainty at times. He has, perhaps, an *idea* of where he's going but not the *feel* of it; in leaving familiar patterns of behaviour for new ones, he sometimes feels false; too much as though he's 'acting' and not 'being'; the change is not yet working from within and can't be taken for granted. The instinctive reaction is then to go back to familiar patterns of behaviour to avoid feeling false and so the movement towards the role is partially blocked or arrested. Because of the nature of this breakdown in self-communication, panic and worry can set in and the block seem insurmountable; it affects everything – meaning, physical response, vocal use, the whole of your motivational equipment and the reason for the character's being. It's a sickening moment. One thing is sure, this state isn't one you can fight your way out of; the more you try to force things the more blocked you become. You have to allow yourself assimilation time and you have to maintain a state which allows you to assimilate. Directorial advice at such times is often along the lines of 'Just let it happen' or 'Relax and it'll come to you', 'Let go a bit and try again'. Good advice. But *how* do you let go? By re-affirming the head/neck/back relationship (see Body Use). The point is that when you are in a consciously well-ordered unhabit-ridden condition you clear the kinaesthetic channels and you can take in, and assimilate, the new information which the changes imposed by the role are in the process of feeding your imagination.

Undoing the block

The skilful director will find various ways of taking pressure off the actor so that his imagination is released into action, because in the end it's the imagination working upon the body which produces the empathetic state in which the change occurs. But sometimes directors are less than helpful and can be downright obstructive of the process they wish to happen. In a production of a large-cast play I was working on, an experienced actor became badly stuck during the later stages of rehearsal when time was running short. The director didn't like his performance and, a brilliant actor himself, showed the actor exactly how to play the part. The actor couldn't do it and became frightened. The pressures upon him were enormous: a world famous actor/director who could make or break his career had to be pleased; he was holding up a huge cast; an understudy was waiting in the wings ready to take over, and the director had already recast several of the smaller roles with understudies and sacked the original actors or relegated them to non-speaking parts. The actor in question agreed with the director's concept of the role, which was excellent and worked well for the play, and he wanted to do it that way; but every time he opened his mouth, despite the fact that he understood the lines perfectly, they came out wrong – sometimes not even making sense.

The first problem was one of translation: the director showed a finished result but didn't show any of the interior processes by which he had arrived at it. So the actor had first to recognize the road which led to the result: he had to find a workable motivation, something other than 'I want to copy what the director does'. So first came understanding. Understanding of itself didn't solve the problem, though. When the actor got back on the stage to rehearse he was so terrified of doing the wrong thing that he was still thinking *how* he should act, so there was no connection between his intention and that of his character. And, too, there was another problem. He started his scene with several loud off-stage yells and his entrance lines were very loud as well. In the normal way his voice served him well enough and he could be clearly heard. Now he was considering *how* to say his lines he began to seize up vocally and was doing considerable damage to himself. This made him all the more frightened. The director's rage and general lack of consideration for the poor actor didn't help either.

By this stage the actor had a clear intellectual understanding of what he needed to do and, because of our work off-stage, of how to do it – that is, how the acting processes could work if allowed to. But he was still in a fix because he lacked the means of breaking the vicious circle 'I am acting – I must get it right – I must concentrate on getting it right – I must work hard and harder to get it right': seize-up.

The outward signs of the seize-up were: a dramatic rise in body temperature, a forced croaking voice, a contracted neck, iron-hard abdominal muscles and quiveringly tense legs; the great blood vessels of the neck were congested, and its whole musculature corded with effort.

At this stage we went back to fundamentals and worked to release the neck and back and reassert the basic freedoms which come from a good head/neck/back relationship. Then, in a cooler condition, we quietly walked the scene through, remembering the motivations for the lines and actions and describing them narratively as if they had been performed by someone else. 'He' rather than 'I'. But all the time we were keeping the head/neck/back relationship working well and refusing the habitual terror-stricken responses. Then, still refusing to tighten into panic, still keeping the head/neck/back relationship going, we went through the scene acting it. It was immediately apparent that a huge change had taken place. The actor no longer looked hounded, he no longer seemed to be trying hard. He had gained in authority. He was taking his own time, and he was aware of his space and of the other actors in it. He was reacting with them. He was actually enjoying himself. And his voice was free and functioning responsively. In fact, he wasn't playing the scene exactly as the director had demonstrated it. He'd begun to live the part and this had brought its own revelation of meaning. However, the director insisted that the scene be played exactly as demonstrated. At this point the actor had a spasm of fright again and began to show signs of getting back into his fixed state. Then he remembered to free his neck and stopped for a moment to do this. Afterwards he was able to go on and achieve exactly what the director wanted. The journey of absorbing consciously-arrived-at-knowledge to the point where it was unselfconsciously useable had been achieved.

The freeing-up process is conscious. It is the fact that it is a conscious process which makes it so valuable when the strange behaviours dredged up from the subconscious make the actor feel adrift from himself. It creates the necessary conditions under which the actor can allow other conscious and subconscious knowledge to work for him. In this instance the actor knew what he had to do, understood it, and needed to be able to trust in the possibility of that knowledge and understanding working for him. So two processes were going on at the same time: the actor was telling himself to free his neck, allowing his head to balance freely and his back to open *and* he was pursuing the objectives of the scene with full and focused energy. What he was not doing was allowing his habitual fearful response to take control, in the way it inevitably did without a conscious refusal to tighten the neck and so on. The acting state and the well-ordered state coexisted in him. 'Learn your acting techniques in order to be able to forget them' is advice often heard in the theatre. That's right. If you have to juggle in a scene you can't spend energy *learning* how to juggle as you do it – consciously working it out. Neither can you afford to devote yourself to working out how to produce your voice during the scene. But during both the learning of these skills and during their employment you can allow yourself to keep your good use going; this in turn will make the learning and the use of these skills easier. It will also increase your general awareness of what is happening to you and around you. It provides the means whereby you can give your performance and monitor it at the same time.

Opening out and projection

Some actors rehearse right from the beginning with the audience in mind and treat the rehearsal space as if it were a theatre. Most go through a stage of development where they are more concerned with getting it right for themselves first and play the action at the size of the rehearsal space while the director and stage manager become, in effect, eavesdroppers. The actor's imagination is at work on making the world of the play as real for himself as possible and he excludes everything and everybody which isn't part of that world. The need to do this is particularly evident in naturalistic plays; but even in narrative theatre, or verse plays, or musicals, the half-private working of the part is often felt to be necessary. An exact knowledge of the self of the play and how that self relates to the other people in the world of the play has to be arrived at and assimilated before the actor starts to open the part out to include an audience. Some actors leave the opening out process until too late and find the sudden presence of the audience, in a much larger space than the rehearsal room, calls for so much adjustment that they temporarily lose their sense of the reality of the world of the play. The adjustment towards including the audience needs to be well under way before the play goes into the theatre. For the voice this is particularly true. Producing enough voice to fill the theatre is something which should happen as part of projecting the whole performance. The objectively arrived at data about character and situation, which the actor has spent considerable energy and time on assimilating so that they have become the subjective truth of the character, now have to be given back in an act of communication with the audience.

Projection is the realized intention to share the world of the play with the audience. It's a communicative interaction which the performer guides. There is a change of energy direction and focus as the actor's intention to share the experience with the audience begins to manifest itself. The voice is louder; this in itself demands more energy, and the increase in energy spreads through the whole performance. The actor's need now is not just to reach the audience but to include them. He needs to be so aware of its moment-by-moment reactions to what is going on that he can adjust his performance from moment to moment to keep the audience imaginatively in the world of the play. Because he needs to receive as well as impart information, he can't afford to start pushing his performance at the audience – if he does he'll probably tighten up and become less receptive. That's why projection isn't just making a loud enough noise or large enough gestures to reach the back row. It's not something the actor does to or at the audience – it's something he does with them.

From the audience's point of view the actor moves and makes noise, and the noise and movement have meaning which illuminate the human condition they share with the actor. It's through his *intention* that his performance reaches, includes and entertains the audience so that this can happen; it's heightened awareness with direction.

Costume and make-up

At some stage in rehearsal you will have a costume fitting. Make sure the costume allows you to breathe and permits such freedom of movement as you need. High collars shouldn't be so high that they make you throw your head back and squash your throat. Corsets and bodices should still allow rib movement in the back and not provoke clavicular breathing and the lack of support that goes with it. Your wig must be securely fitted so that you're not spending your time balancing it and getting a tight neck in the process. If you wear a make-up moustache or beard make sure it's well stuck on; it's surprisingly common to find actors who've choked on a moustache during performance because the glue didn't hold when they were taking a breath.

Into the theatre

When you move into the theatre from the rehearsal room you will need to take account of the changed acoustic. Not only is the theatre likely to be much larger than the space in which you rehearsed, but it will do different things to the sound of your voice. You need to get on the stage as soon as you can and listen to the way the theatre absorbs or reflects your voice. As the technical and dress rehearsals are under way, try sitting in various parts of the theatre to see if there are 'dead spots' where it's difficult to hear what's going on. Try, in a word, to judge how much volume you're going to need. The acoustic properties of the theatre will change as you get the set on stage and they'll change again when you have an audience, particularly if it's a full house; experience will show you the changes you need to make under these changing conditions, but any feedback you can get from front of house staff is likely to be helpful. (See also Trying to Fill the Space.)

Warming up

If it's possible, and the stage manager allows, it's good to do your warm-up on stage, while it's still open to the auditorium. A company warm-up is often the most helpful kind, but it's surprising how many actors fight shy of warm-ups and, unless the director calls the warm-up, it's quite usual to find actors sticking in the dressing room and either not warming up at all physically and vocally, or making a few token noises just to make sure the 'tubes are clear'. I mention this because it can be quite intimidating if you want to warm up and those around you don't. You may find you have to do most of your warm-up before you arrive at the theatre. (See An Actor's Warm-Up.)

Radio

Radio drama has been called 'the theatre of the skull' and it's a good description. The audience has only sound and imagination to work with in realizing the play's images, characters, relationships and changes of place and time. Radio demands close listening. This being so, once the convention of the piece has been established, any falsity or lack of truth in the actors' performances is quickly detected – there is no distraction, no physical spectacle – every sound will contribute something to the audience's imagined world of the play including sounds which shouldn't be there – coughs, the rustle of pages being turned and so on. The microphone is not as selective as the ear. In ordinary life we make a continuing assessment of what is relevant to our listening and shut out the sounds which are not. The microphone can't do this.

Radio is a fast medium and shifts its ground like lightning between scene and scene, so the actor may find he's playing extreme anguish at one moment and three seconds later is making light-hearted dinner table chat.

The range of emotions called for in radio is likely to be as great as in the theatre, but the expression of them is different. The intensity remains but the volume of vocal expression is often necessarily less. Radio is primarily a close-up medium; this leads to a 'pressure cooker' effect in the acting, particularly in soliloquy, or when the character's thoughts are being overheard, as it were. Some sounds which in theatre acting might have less significance – the quality of breathing for example – become very important in radio. And the use of pause is extremely important. In the theatre there's still a lot to see during a pause; on radio the audience has to imagine what's going on, so the pause becomes a great builder of suspense.

There are technical problems caused by the need for different actors to maintain the same distance from the microphone, and in a large-cast play this can lead to a complicated dance as actors exchange places, keep their scripts from rustling, and avoid bumping into each other and making extraneous noises. Often this quadrille has to be worked out in detail in rehearsal. And none of this must for one moment take the actor out of the imaginary world he is creating.

Before you arrive at the studio there's a certain amount of preparation to be done. Try to get hold of the script as soon as possible. Rehearsal time for a radio play tends to be short. Sometimes programmes which are not plays but have dramatized parts in them are rehearsed and recorded in the same short session. So if your part calls for a vocal change you must work it out at home until it sounds completely natural – use a tape recorder to check. Choose your clothes with the microphone in mind and avoid those which rustle or creak, and squeaky shoes. (It's quite a good idea to ask the producer whether you should wear hard or soft shoes; you may find the noise of your footsteps is to be heard.) When you get to the studio make sure you're not covered in clanking jewellery and leave metal money, key rings etc. away from the microphone. The studio is often a dry airless place and provokes dry mouth. If you suffer from this, provide yourself with a cup of water (or a lemon) in advance, but place it out of range of the microphone. You will probably find that you don't need all of the script; in this case, discard what you can; radio script paper is heavy and holding a huge script for an hour or two can lead to accidental noises; page turning, down and away from the microphone, can be difficult to do without noise; if you're not used to it give it some practice. Have a pencil and eraser ready for script changes; often scripts have to be doctored to allow for exits and entrances and that means providing an extra line or two. I have found it useful in the past to have a Pronouncing Dictionary with me. Producers are usually helpful when it comes to the pronunciation of unusual or foreign words, and in the BBC there is a Pronunciation Unit to supply them with information, but having the dictionary handy sometimes saves the time of a telephone call to the Unit.

Microphone acting (radio, dubbing, voice-overs and the like) is, of all forms of acting, that which relies most on the voice, and yet, in its way, it's as physical as any other form of acting. Changes of emotion, the playing of any character, do not just happen in the vocal tract. Acting demands the involvement of the entire person; if you think of microphone acting as just a voice job, it's likely to sound cerebral and illustrative rather than active – as if you're giving us a token of what character or emotion is called for rather than the thing itself. Radio recording and production techniques have changed a good deal over the last few years and now quite often 'sets' are built in the recording studio and actors may be called upon to move while they are acting, and it's quite usual to see a lot of movement in a studio. But even if this kind of movement is denied the actor, he must still allow himself the physical changes which character, situation and emotion demand. Eye contact is important in feeding your performance and keeping it alive and it helps to liberate you from the cramping effect on the voice which occurs when you're stuck in the script all the time. It helps if you know your lines fairly well.

At about a foot from the microphone it's as if you were a foot from the listener's ear; at two feet from the microphone it's as if you were four feet from his ear. This means that you normally work within a fairly small space range. Practice lets you become adept at knowing how near to the microphone you need to be. During rehearsal these distances will be worked out – note them down. If you fluff, and all actors do from time to time, you will have to go back and re-record; it's vital for voice-levels that you know *where* you should be in relation to the microphone. When you fluff, just go back, well beyond the point at which you fluffed, and don't bother to apologize – everyone knows you're sorry it happened –

apologies waste time and get you out of the rhythm of the play and its imaginative ambience, and keeping that going is the prime task.

Often reactions are not scripted but have to be heard, and, too, you may have to make the appropriate noises for eating and drinking, and so on. This can lead to some bizarre and unbelievable results at times. These 'effects' noises need to be done with discretion or you may end up making a bad advertisement for the activity rather than suggesting the activity is actually going on. To hear some actors making 'I am getting up from an armchair' noises you might suppose they were about to suffer a heart attack. When actors make bad sound effects it's quite often because they haven't spent enough time listening to what the noises of real life are like.

If you have to speak over pre-recorded sound to a Q-light, it's a good idea to make sure you hear the recording beforehand. As you hear the recording of a storm at sea, a battle, the lazy drone of insects on a hot summer afternoon or whatever it is, your imagination will work with it and your voice automatically adjust. You can call that to mind when you record and perhaps cannot actually hear the pre-recorded sound. If you've never heard the sound which is supposed to be the background noise of your scene, your voice probably won't carry the full awareness of the situation.

Talks and interviews

It's normal for people in the public eye to be put in the public ear as well. These suggestions are for people who are likely to find themselves at the sharp end of an interview or being asked to give a talk on radio. If you are giving a talk it helps if you imagine one specific person and talk to the microphone as if it were that person. Imagining you are talking to the public at large produces a falsely rhetorical effect which is at odds with the medium. In preparing the script for your talk it may help in preserving an unstudied spontaneous effect if you have first actually *talked* it, into a tape recorder, and then typed that up as your script. The usages of the written word differ mightily from those of speech. Interviews are usually easier from the speaker's point of view because there is actually a person present, usually on the other side of the table, to whom you can talk. Telephone interviews are more difficult, especially if you haven't a good line; avoid the tendency to shout. Talk as normally as you can. When long-distance interviews take place with the interviewer in one studio and you in another wearing a set of headphones so that you can hear his voice, there's a tendency to want to raise the voice. This should be resisted. Talk to the microphone as if it were the interviewer.

Film and television

Voice use in film and television is radically different from its use in the theatre. Nearly all film acting is as naturalistic as it's possible to get, while the theatre uses naturalism only from time to time. And in the theatre the naturalistic approach is modified by the necessity to project the performance to the audience. In filming, it's as if there is no audience while you act, and your projection is only to the other actors in your scenes. Also on stage you have to edit the naturalistic response so as not to lose the shape and pace of the scene, and your hold on the audience's attention; in film the editing is done in the cutting room. Since naturalistic behaviour is called for, you don't have to concern yourself with maximizing your resonance or with the other artifices you employ in the theatre to make the voice carry so the audience can hear it as if it were 'natural'; in film it must be natural.

The energy in screen acting is more contained than in theatre acting. Even in medium close-up the camera picks up the smallest nuances of behaviour. Screen acting is not a withdrawal of vitality; you still need total commitment to the moment of action and a strongly motivated inner life for the role, because that, more than anything else, is what the camera will be seeking – it's as if it reads your thoughts. Keeping that interior life of the character going and sustaining the imagined world of the scene is the prime task; and it needs to be done despite the many distractions of the moment.

On the floor of the set it often seems that technical considerations are paramount. Technicians are forever adjusting lights, your make-up is touched up just as you are about to shoot, props checked around you – and all while you are trying to keep 'in character' and sustain the believability of your inner world. The shooting schedule is important and everyone wants the scene in the can as soon as possible so the next shot can be set up. Sometimes it may seem that the actors are an afterthought – a few hurried words of advice from the director and then: 'Camera's rolling', crack goes the clapperboard, the director calls 'Action!', and you're off.

Dubbing, looping and voice-overs

A good deal of what I've said about acting for radio applies in the dubbing or voice-over studio, but the circumstances are usually more difficult. Often you are the only actor present; the recording area may be cramped and you have so many things to take care of that it's easy to be thrown and tighten up and lose effective judgement and control.

Dubbing is the laying down of a voice track to picture. The film is run in loops with a vertical line moving across the screen; at the moment it reaches the right hand edge of the screen you begin talking. The loop is continuous and usually of a fairly short piece of film, so you can watch it a few times to get the synchronization of your speech and the picture (lip-synch). But your time isn't unlimited; dubbing studios cost a lot and there's always a sense of pressure to get the loop done as soon as possible. Ignore it. You have to concentrate on recreating the imaginative process behind the line.

If you are dubbing a foreign language film into English you are trying to create vocally the character which someone else has already given a great deal of thought to. You have to empathize with that other actor's characterization until you have the feel of the person. On a large-budget film perhaps the director will rehearse you into the role. Often you will only have the assistance of the dubbing director; which in most cases means a technician who is more concerned about lip-synch, and sound levels, than the acting. Allow your empathy with the image to be as complete as possible. This will mean that cramped behind your acoustic screens with the microphone and your lectern and the film loop running on a big screen a few feet in front of you, you begin to move according to the emotion and the character. The movements are small – you can't move with the freedom of the person on the screen because you have to stay near the microphone; they amount to little more than token postures – but these are the outward signs of an inner involvement with the character and its emotions, so let them happen; they help you achieve the right quality of sound. In fact it's with this physical change to another state of being that the whole process of producing the voice in a manner which will credibly match the image of what the character on screen is doing begins. (See Voice and Movement.)

Looping your own screen performance is a similar process. But here you at least have the advantage of knowing how you arrived at the sound the character is making on the screen. You are probably doing the loops because during filming there was background noise or the acoustics were poor. In this case you will be asked to repeat your previous performance and that shouldn't be too difficult. Sometimes, however, the exigencies of the shooting schedule have meant that the director has accepted a take which isn't quite what he wants. It looks fine, but the way you delivered the line wasn't good enough. In that case you have a juggling act to do. Physically your character is doing one thing on the screen and now the director is asking you for something different vocally. This can be a frustrating business, and it's a good time to think of freeing your neck, because every instinct will ask you to match the physical expression with the vocal, i.e. to do what you did before. Probably it's a question of nuance, but it might mean a radical rethink of the scene. Stay free, and don't hesitate to ask the director to work you through it before you do the take.

Voice-overs are a different business and may not call for much in the way of your acting skills. If you're narrating a documentary film, for example, your talents as a writer are likely to be more in demand. Documentary scripts are often ineptly written. They are written 'to picture', that is, a certain amount of information has to be conveyed during a specific sequence of film. This often leads documentary script writers into strange syntax and stranger juxtapositions of words, and the results can be almost unspeakable except by a vocal contortionist. If you can find a direct and simple way of saying what has to be said, suggest it – probably the script writer will be grateful. Usually the recording session will be in a small studio; you will be put in an airless box with a table and a microphone and a glass of water. Through a glass panel you will be able to see the film either on a television-sized monitor or, if you're lucky, on a large screen. There will also be a footage counter. The footage numbers are marked in the left margin of your script so you know by watching the counter roughly how long you have before you're due to speak. About ten feet before you're due to speak you should release your neck and allow in the breath you'll need. Staying released while you're recording is important; if you're not, it will be evident in the voice – minute trembles in the tone, irregular or exaggerated inflexion patterns begin to show as your worry colours the words. If you fluff, calmly go back. The projectionist will wind back and you have time while that's being done to sort out the problem. If you feel, in retrospect, that you could have handled some of the script better, say so. It's nearly always possible to make a wild-track (not to picture) recording of alternatives.

Preparation for a recording session is important. You should sort out the problems in the script – such as rewrites, pronunciations, your attitude in interpreting the text, before the session really gets under way. Over a coffee you can discuss these points with the director. Take a Pronouncing Dictionary, pencils and erasers to the session. Your physical preparation is even more important. Make sure you've got your voice working well before you arrive at the studio. If it's a morning session and your voice takes an hour or two to settle after sleep, make sure you've got up early enough to give it a thorough workout before you start; you must have your voice absolutely under control for recording sessions. The equipment registers the finest details. If you're short of breath on a long phrase it will sound like it. The microphone is no more, usually, than a foot from your mouth as you speak; if you're given to over-exploding consonants or hissing the sibilant sounds it will show. Go through the script before you arrive at the studio and note any places where difficulty of phrasing may lead you into this kind of speech fault – if possible, of course, change the script – but if you can't do that at least you'll be prepared for the worst.

An actor's warm-up

A warm-up before performance isn't a thorough workout. It presupposes that basically you're in a fit enough state to do the job, and most of your physical preparation will have been done earlier during the rehearsal period or as a matter of course during your everyday routine. It is what its name suggests. Before a performance all you should need to do by way of preparation is ensure that you're feeling physically limber and supple, that your voice is well tuned for the demands of the role and that mentally you're attuned to the theatre and the world of the play. Part of this is best done in the theatre, on stage if possible. The first part can be done anywhere reasonably quiet.

Release

Before you get on with tuning yourself up to play your role you should find time for a short session devoted to releasing your body and mind from the everyday tensions which are inclined to take a grip on one. Half-an-hour's relaxation or a short nap might work. I find this makes me sluggish and it takes me a long time to get in a fit state for work thereafter. A solution which seems to work well for most actors who have tried it is to spend about fifteen minutes on the floor, on your back, with your knees up, your head supported on books to a comfortable height while you direct the joints to release and open, and work on your head/neck/back relationship (see Body Use: Floor Work). As the body opens out and the breathing regularizes, there is a sense of quiet, contained energy and mental alertness. This is the state you want to be in, and it happens because you allow it to happen rather than because you're trying to make it happen. Once this state is achieved, mentally run through the job ahead without allowing this to tighten your neck or affect your breathing; the natural anxiety or excitement in the anticipation of the performance mustn't be allowed to spoil your state of energetic equilibrium. Having reviewed the work ahead, begin to tune the voice, fairly gently and quietly, working particu- larly to feel the resonance buzz the whole body (see Body Buzz). For this you could use humming or vowel sequences. By the time you've finished this floor work your voice should be resonating fully and easily. If it isn't, try the Whispered 'Ah'. This will quickly open the throat and get your breathing going. Then resonate the 'Ah' paying particular attention to releasing the jaw and tongue-root and to economy of air-flow. Check with a finger on the lips, as usual. Now work through alternate humming and extended vowels, [ɑ:, u:, i:], until full resonance with release is achieved.

On stage

When you get on stage, if that is where you're going to warm up, do a few exercises to get the circulation and breathing into a more energetic use. After floor work your joints should be open and fairly supple. You can get your circulation and breathing working with some running on the spot but don't let this, or any other exercise you may choose to do, bring you away from the good head/neck/back relationship. When you begin to feel warm, start jumps, then jumps with turns, and stretching movements. Follow this with a short burst of Blowing Out Candles and Conducting the Orchestra (see p. 57 and p. 53). Now feel out the acoustic quality of the theatre, making loud and quiet noises, perhaps using a vowel phrase such as 'How are you', always checking the economy of breath use. Don't stop moving when doing this; try the sound with your back to the auditorium, facing the wings, facing front. You'll notice that when you speak facing certain directions (different according to the kind of set you have) your voice seems to be more absorbed and lacks ring; this will be particularly true if you talk towards heavy drapes, for example. See if you can talk and turn in a circle and keep the ring in the voice. Keep re-affirming the head/neck/back relationship. Now, standing stage centre, if you can, and facing front, talk, or make a short speech, while allowing your consciousness to expand until it includes the whole of the theatre; pay particular attention to your back, to what is behind you; then to what space is above you and below you; finally to the space in front of you. As you mentally open up to include all this space, your throat should feel wide open, your neck quite free, and you will be using your whole back to breathe, with a marked movement of the ribs from armpit level down. Now, just talking easily, your voice should be comfortably filling the theatre with great economy of breath-flow. Put that economy to the test with a couple of the more difficult consonant Practice Paragraphs.

By this time body and voice are tuned. Anything more you do should be done with the role in mind. Keeping your sense of openness and freedom, walk and talk through a scene, in character. Or improvise in character. When you feel the character and good use of the voice and body have come together you're well warmed up.

Company warm-ups

A company warm-up, providing everyone co-operates, is the best way of warming up for a show. You not only tune up your voice and muscles, you also re-affirm the company identity, the sense that you're all working together to the same end. It can go a long way towards abolishing pre-performance nerves, especially early in the run. What you do in the warm-up will depend upon the kind of show. For a musical with dance, you need a thorough limbering up of the body and it's good to follow the routine the choreographer has used during rehearsal; and for the voice, one of the less demanding songs in the show and perhaps a few scales or the singing of a round such as 'Rose Rose' or 'London's Burning'. In a straight play quite often two or three fast moving games make a good beginning to a warm-up. The Mirror Game is played in pairs; you face each other and one partner initiates the moves while the other partner tries to make a mirror image of them; start slowly and gradually build up speed – it helps if you maintain eye contact. Building a Machine is a game with movement and voice; one person begins by making a repeated pattern of movements and noise; one by one the others join in as different parts of the machine with complementary sounds and movements until the whole company is active. Both of these games are adaptable to the mood of the play. The singing and moving of rounds can be an excellent voice, movement and mood warm-up. 'Rose Rose' lends itself to stately legato movements which can be developed into a simple dance; 'London's Burning' can be moved in a variety of ways, with great urgency, with a heavy stamping rhythm or you can form a chain with the repeated motion of hauling up buckets of water and throwing the water on the fire; or the leader of the round can go through it with a series of movements which the rest of the company adopt as they come into the round. Be sure the round leader is someone who can pitch the song comfortably for everyone, particularly if the song has a wide range of note. After the playing of games and singing of rounds the company should be feeling well warmed up, and it's a good idea then to stop a few minutes before the end of the time allocated so that people can go through their own private preparation if they wish. Before a company warm-up, as before your private warm-up, a certain amount of time spent releasing and ordering the body is good preparation.

For teachers

Teachers seem, as a profession, to be plagued by sore throats and voice loss. Sometimes this is due simply to vocal misuse exacerbated by the nature of the job, and sometimes by environmental hazards. If your voice use as a teacher is inadequate you need first of all to do the general work outlined in the first three sections of the book to make sure your body use, breathing and phonation is working well.

In the classroom

Make sure the room is well ventilated. If you use chalk and a blackboard keep chalk dust down by cleaning the board with a damp duster.

Before the season of coughs and colds begins, take all sensible precautions which recommend themselves to you to avoid catching these diseases. The best general prophylactic against colds and coughs that I know of is a healthy diet rich in Vitamin C, and daily exercise to maintain general fitness, and an anti-flu injection.

In the classroom a great deal of the teacher's energy is used to keep order; often this entails using the voice at great volume. A mature adult can produce enough volume of sound, if the voice is properly produced, to be able to quell, at least temporarily, the rowdiest class. The trouble comes when the teacher momentarily lets go an urgent and violent blast of sound as an unthinking reaction to some troublemaker. It's the unthinking bit that does the damage: you identify the source of trouble, you tighten up and almost throw your head in the direction you're shouting. Better to pause a moment, free the neck and make sure you support the voice as you yell; better because you'll produce a bigger sound, use less energy, not hurt your throat, feel more in control of the situation, and, because your control of the situation will be evident, you'll be more impressive. Of course, if you have managed to pause and free yourself, you may well decide vocal violence is not the best way of achieving attention.

There is also the problem that some teachers face of having to talk for a great deal of the working day. Talking all day can be tiring, but if your body use is good it should certainly be possible to do this without strain. A careful reading of the first three sections of the book and some practice of the basic breathing and tuning exercises will help you develop your vocal equipment to an adequate standard fairly quickly. Try reading aloud one of the consonant Practice Paragraphs with a finger on your lips. If you feel much of an air-flow on your finger the chances are that when you speak loudly, or shout, that air-flow is increased to such a point that the protective mucus on the vocal cords is being dried out and the cords suffering damage as a result. The work on Tuning will put that right. Some of this work can be applied immediately to save you getting the sore throat or voice loss caused by prolonged periods of loud speech, or short bursts of shouting.

Central heating dries the air quickly and this makes prolonged voice use tiring. If you have central heating in your classroom, make sure you have some way of putting humidity back into the atmosphere. Bowls of water on the radiators will serve as well as anything.

Open-air work

If your job calls for you to teach in the open air a lot and this gives you voice strain, get a megaphone; it's kinder to your voice not to push it to its limits and the open air, particularly if there's a breeze blowing the wrong way, is inimical to good voice production; unless there are buildings all round to act as sound reflectors the resonance of the voice will be dispersed and the clarity of the speech lost very quickly. A good megaphone will usually quadruple the effective distance you can reach with your voice. Again, though, reaching with your voice doesn't mean you have to reach with your head; keep the neck quite free and make sure the abdominal muscles are supporting the voice.

Reaction to the cold outside air, especially if you've just come from a heated building, can be unhelpful. If you start shivering and closing up the joints, lifting the shoulders and tightening the neck, you will make the business of producing the voice much more difficult – so stay warm if you can, and if you can't, while you're using your voice at any rate, behave as if you are warm and refuse to allow all that tension, particularly in the neck, shoulders and rib-cage.

Voice care

Strain

The vocal equipment is remarkably resilient and can stand a lot of
misuse without suffering permanent damage, but it's as well not to
put this to the test too often. Repeated patterns of vocal misuse can
lead to irreversible damage, especially a strained use of the cords or
a persistant interference with the breath supply. These two points
shouldn't occur with anyone who is producing his voice in the way
this book advocates. However, short-term strains do occur from
time to time because the voice has, even for a moment or two, been
badly produced – particularly when shouting and screaming is
concerned, or some unaccustomed athleticism of voice use such as
singing in an unfamiliar pitch range without adequate preparation.

If you are intending to use your voice athletically you must make
sure you have prepared for it by giving yourself an adequate warm-
up, or in the case of a substantial pitch change, by doing the relevant
exercises over a period of days beforehand. Muscles are involved
and they need to be gradually accustomed to the extraordinary
workload, or you will suffer voice damage through fatigue. If,
despite all your care, you do overtire or strain the cords and begin
to suffer voice loss, or even that lack of fine control of the nuances
of pitch, volume and timbre which is normal in the fully responsive
voice, you should proceed very carefully: it's now that you can, by
pushing on injudiciously, make matters so bad that you will need
medical propping-up to give your performance. This can be costly
and is not always good for the voice in the long run. If you can,
when you strain the voice, either stop using it for however long it
takes for the damage to right itself, or at least use the voice quietly
until you get a chance to rest. Then, lie down, if possible on a gently
inclined plane with your head lower than your feet, and give yourself
half-an-hour of relaxed rest; make sure you're completely warm
when you do this. In the case of minor strain and fatigue this can
have a splendidly regenerative effect; but use your voice with care
for the rest of the day all the same.

In all cases of damage resulting from temporary misuse of the
voice the best treatment is rest and silence. If you must give
a performance and you've badly strained the voice, consult a
laryngologist and preferably one who specializes in working with

singers and actors. He may alleviate your symptoms and bring the voice back into a temporarily usable condition. But such treatment will often mean you will need longer rest to recuperate the voice afterwards. One warning: the onset of voice loss through fatigue, once it shows itself in aches of the throat muscles, and the anchorage of the tongue and the neck, is probably well on the way; the small intrinsic muscles of the larynx usually do not give much pain as they are overworking and by the time the strain has begun to be felt in the larger muscles of the throat you've probably already done considerable damage. Stop. Rest. Give yourself a good release session and, if possible, don't use the voice till the following day. You should then try to work out what you are doing which produces this strain and work another way to avoid doing it again.

Coughs, colds and throat infections

A persistant dry cough is best treated by a laryngologist. There is a great variety of patent medicines available for the treatment of colds, flu, coughs, catarrh (whatever that is) and the different varieties of nasal, bronchial and laryngeal troubles which tend to beset us, particularly during the winter months; most of them are junk, some are dangerous, a few help in alleviating symptoms. Particularly to be avoided by professional voice users are any medicines which promise to dry up mucus. You need mucus to lubricate your larynx and if you haven't got it and are using the voice at stretch you will damage the cords. I have used such preparations in the past both on stage and when recording a voice-over; the immediate relief of congestion and thick mucus secretion obtained led to a dry throat in both cases and a persistent throat irritation. On stage this was more of a nuisance than the cold; in the recording booth it didn't matter so much because the recording could be stopped while I coughed and it did mean that I could match the voice quality of part of the sound-track which had been recorded before I got the cold.

As yet medical opinion on the treatment of colds is divided; some hold to the theory that massive intake of Vitamin C prevents, or at any rate lessens, your likelihood of catching cold. Others say claims for Vitamin C in this case are exaggerated. I take it and hope. If I have a severe throat infection with voice loss, and I'm working, I go to see the laryngologist. One preventive which has seemed helpful to me is an injection at the beginning of winter against flu. (When I remember in time, I get this injection from my homoeopathic doctor; so far whenever I have had the injection I haven't caught flu during the subsequent winter.)

Smoking

From the voice point of view it would seem that some professional speakers can smoke moderately without suffering damage to the voice in the short term, while others cannot take tobacco at all without immediate impairment of vocal efficiency. If you feel tobacco is doing your voice harm and intend to stop smoking it is best to do so when you are not working. Most smokers who stop go through a period of vocal adjustment during which the voice often sounds worse than before. Eventually, the change-over complete, the voice regains its clarity and the efficiency in tuning generally improves a good deal. The longer-term effects of smoking on the voice are insidious and you are not likely to be aware of them until quite suddenly you find you haven't the necessary breath control. Deposits of tar in the lungs cut down your oxygen absorption and eventually this can lead to shortness of breath. Heavy smokers will in due course suffer some deterioration in the condition of the cords and this will affect their ability to tune the voice, particularly in the higher range. A special word of caution to pipe smokers: some so get into the habit of clenching the teeth that this affects voice and speech (even when the pipe isn't in the mouth); pipe smokers should, therefore, pay particular attention to the jaw release work.

Alcohol

Heavy spirit drinking leads to cordal damage as does heavy smoking. Alcohol before a performance is not a good idea; if you drink enough to raise your body temperature you're drinking enough to provoke extra blood flow to the vocal cords; it will have an effect on your tuning and may cause you to produce a rougher sound than normal.

Dry mouth

Anxiety sometimes lessens the secretion of saliva and the thin mucus which lubricates the larynx and throat. Work on the head/neck/

back relationship may tackle this at its root and will certainly help to get stage fright under control (see Stage Fright). However, you may still be suffering from a dry mouth – suck a slice of lemon or smell some vinegar; glasses of water don't really help. Lemon is particularly helpful if you're working in a dry atmosphere. It's an odd and sometimes physically distressing fact that actors spend most of their working lives in atmospheres which are unhelpful to the vocal equipment. Theatres, film and television studios, radio studios and recording booths nearly always have dry overheated atmospheres; this can cause dry mouth even without the anxiety.

Nodules on the cords

I have never known of a case of nodules on the vocal cords that was not caused by bad voice use. If your laryngologist diagnoses them and advises their surgical removal, wait before agreeing to the operation. Try first to find out what has been wrong with your use. Sometimes nodules do disappear when the larynx is given rest. After the operation for removal of nodules on the cords you will have to rest the voice for a long time anyway, so you might as well see what effect resting the cords has before committing yourself to surgery. And in any case, if the nodules are not to reappear, even after the most successful surgery, you *must* find out what caused them and take steps to retrain your voice use so that you do not go on damaging yourself.

Laryngologists

Sometimes there is a crisis: your voice is failing fast and you have a performance to give. In such an emergency you need a laryngologist, and preferably one who has specialized in working with actors and singers, someone who is experienced in the matter of propping up ailing voices in the critical situation of performance, and someone who understands the special pressures under which an actor lives. There are various preparations, which need skill in administering, which a singers' or actors' laryngologist is more likely to have to hand in a crisis than anyone else. Quite often your local GP will not know about such preparations and will be only moderately skilled in administering them even if he does know what to prescribe. Also a laryngologist who concerns himself with theatre people is more likely to make himself available for consultation when *you* need him – often at inconvenient times.

For further reading about voice care I recommend *The Singer's and Actor's Throat* by Norman Punt (Heinemann).

APPENDICES

Appendix 1: Breathing: A Brief Anatomy

The lungs

The lungs, and heart, occupy most of the interior space of the rib-cage; this space is called the thoracic cavity; its walls are the ribs and its floor is the diaphragm. The principal function of the lungs is to oxygenate the blood and remove certain gaseous wastes from the body, principally carbon dioxide. A secondary function, but all important for the voice user, is to supply the outward going air-flow which acts as conveyor of the voice. We do not have direct control of the lungs; but we have effective control, because although the lungs are not attached to the rib-cage or the diaphragm, they always move to follow the shape these impose on the thoracic cavity.

The nerves

Basically the process of breathing is activated by a cyclical action of the phrenic nerve and the vagus nerve. The phrenic nerve activates the diaphragm to descend and flatten; the lungs expand to fill the space because of the negative pressures created. In doing this, the phrenic nerve is joined by the lower six intercostal nerves, so the diaphragm acts, as it were, with a fail-safe system. Once the lungs reach a certain stage of expansion, the vagus nerve, by means of its pressure receptors in the lungs, receives the information that the lungs are in danger of being over-stretched and transmits this information back to the respiratory centres in the brain which cause inhalation to stop and exhalation to take its place. This cyclical activity, the rhythmicity in breathing referred to on pp. 43–4, responds to information fed to the respiratory centres by the higher inputs of the brain, such as emotional activity, and the desire to speak and phrase our speech, for example, and so to some extent is capable of conscious control. One of the main points in working on breathing is to ensure that this cyclical activity remains properly functioning. Once it breaks down we are in trouble; we can cause it to break down by breathing in too much or by forcing the out-breath too far, or by fixing the breathing muscles in a state of spasm.

The muscles

The principal muscles used in breathing are the diaphragm, the abdominal muscles and the muscles of the ribs. The diaphragm is a large sheet of muscle attached to the end of the breast bone, the spine and the upper pair of the floating ribs. If you trace the line of your ribs from the breast bone back to the spine you will be following the curve of the diaphragm and its line of attachment. You will see it is at its lowest in the back where the lobes of the lungs reach down towards the kidneys. So the opening of the back during inspiration is important if we wish to use the lungs to the fullest. Working together with the diaphragm and the abdominal muscles are the intercostal or rib muscles and these have the function of elevating and depressing the ribs during inhalation and exhalation; when you breathe out, one set of rib muscles pulls the ribs closed, when you breathe in, another set of rib muscles pulls the ribs open. The abdominal muscle you will be most aware of in breathing is rectus abdominis which attaches at its lowest point to the pelvic girdle at the pubis symphysis and extends upwards in a broad sheet to attach to the lower ribs in front. This muscle, with others, has the job of protecting the viscera. During the in-breath it releases and during the out-breath it contracts and assists in depressing the ribs; while it is doing this it is also causing a displacement of the viscera upwards into the rib-cage, thus supporting the upward movement of the diaphragm.

The bones

Those we are most concerned with are the ribs, the spine and the breast bone, although during the act of breathing it is sometimes important to note what is happening to the collar bones, the shoulder blades, and, indeed the bones of the legs and arms. All of the ribs are articulated in the back with two of the vertebrae, from which they take a path that curves forward and down towards the front of the rib-cage where the first seven ribs attach directly to the breast bone; the next three share the same line of attachment via their fused cartilages which form one point of attachment to the breast bone; the final two pairs of ribs have only an attachment to the spine and are called floating ribs. The ribs are capable of a rotary motion during elevation and depression at their points of articulation; however, not all of the ribs have the same degree of flexibility of movement; here the lower ribs definitely have an advantage. The largest lateral movement in the rib-cage is in the lower half. The rib-cage is also capable of an up and down movement and moves to follow the curves of the spine as they change. (In addition, muscles in the neck may be employed to pull the whole rib-cage and the collar bones upwards. This happens during clavicular breathing, and various kinds of nervous and hysterical behaviour may provoke this movement as well. On the whole it is unnecessary for our purposes and does not materially help the breath supply as long as the head/neck/back relationship is working efficiently.)

Appendix 2: F. M. Alexander

Frederick Matthias Alexander was born in 1869 in Tasmania. From an early age he was interested in acting and public recitation. At the age of twenty he went to Melbourne to seek some training with money he had saved from various jobs for that purpose. When his savings ran out he continued his studies of acting and the violin by supporting himself as before. Whatever the job, he made sure that his evenings were free for acting and directing plays. He also began to put together a repertoire of comic and serious pieces for recitation. The Reciter at this time offered one of the most popular forms of available entertainment, and by all accounts, Alexander had a considerable gift for it. Certainly by the age of twenty-five he had established himself in Australia as a successful performer and he undertook a tour of New Zealand.

For some time there had been a tendency for his voice to fail him during performance and he was constantly plagued by vocal strain and sore throats. Medical examination could show no adequate cause for this and the remedies which were suggested to him and which Alexander tried produced no better result than a slight alleviation of symptoms. His voice continued to suffer and the condition was clearly a threat to his career. Alexander made a deduction, simple enough in itself, but of revolutionary implications: since his voice normally functioned well and only failed when he came to perform, there must be something which he was doing during performance that caused the trouble. If this were the case, no amount of medication was likely to help.

In an attempt to pin-point the cause of the voice failure, Alexander began a lengthy process of self-observation. He also made an intensive study of the breathing methods then generally in vogue for professional voice users, and concluded that they offered no solution to his particular problem. What did lead to a solution was his observation that in opening his mouth to speak he tilted his head back, thereby making a slight shortening in his neck which in turn led to a poor use of the breathing mechanism. In producing the necessary volume of sound for performing, this was exaggerated. But because this head-tilt was habitually attached to the act of speaking, it had to be corrected for ordinary everyday speech as well for performance.

Alexander's approach to the problem of habitual response was refined and changed during the months that followed the original discovery of the interference that was affecting his voice. As he developed his observations into practice, changing his use of the body and removing his habitual responses to the act of speaking, his voice use so improved that actors, reciters and singers wished to study his method of voice production and he became much sought after as a teacher. He was so successful as a teacher that he decided to make teaching his career. He moved from Auckland to Melbourne, concentrated on developing his technique, and soon had a large practice teaching it.

Early on Alexander had realized the fuller implications of what he was doing and by now his method of teaching was to work on the 'Use of the self'; the use of voice and breathing was a natural development from this and not something to be worked on apart. This led in some of his pupils to improvements in functions other than voice use. Eventually, as these non-vocal benefits became known, a local doctor sent his son, who suffered from pulmonary tuberculosis, for lessons. He followed this up by sending a patient who suffered from adhesions of the lungs. Another doctor sent a patient with spinal trouble. Soon, Alexander was accepting more pupils from the medical profession than from the theatre, and various members of the Melbourne University Medical Faculty were among his pupils as well.

Alexander had not given up his association with the theatre. In 1899 he moved to Sydney and established his teaching practice there. He also became director of the Sydney Dramatic and Operatic Conservatorium from 1900 to 1904. One of his friends in Sydney was Dr J. W. Steward McKay, famous for his work as a surgeon at Lewisham Hospital. McKay had been convinced of the great value of Alexander's work, particularly in gynaecological cases; often his work had prevented the need for surgery. McKay encouraged

Alexander to move to London, which, as the capital of the British Empire, was an inevitable choice if his work was to become as well known as it merited.

Armed with medical and theatrical introductions, in 1904 Alexander set up his practice in London. At first most of his pupils were drawn from the theatre and he worked with many of the great actors of his day, including Sir Henry Irving, Beerbohm-Tree and Lewis Waller. He worked and lived until 1910 in the Army and Navy Mansions, Victoria Street; thereafter his London address was at 16 Ashley Place SW1.

By 1910 it had become necessary for Alexander to publish. His work was widespread in its influence, much talked about, and beginning to be misrepresented; there was also the threat of plagiarism. A definitive statement of the principles of the work was needed. Alexander wrote and published *Man's Supreme Inheritance*. It continued in print for the next forty-five years.

In 1914 Alexander visited the United States and from then until 1924 he spent half of each year in both countries. The practices in London and New York were kept going with the help of assistants. In 1923 Alexander published his second book *Constructive Conscious Control of the Individual*. In 1930 a training course for teachers of his method was established. And in 1932 *The Use of Self* was published as an account of what Alexander himself had done to work out his technique.

Alexander's achievements as a teacher had inspired one of his assistants, Miss Irene Tasker, to found a school for young children. In general the school followed a normal curriculum but was unique in concentrating on how the children used themselves while learning. In 1940, shortly after the outbreak of war, the school and Alexander – now in his seventies – moved to the United States. The work had been kept alive in America by, among others, A. R. Alexander, F.M.'s brother. In 1943 Alexander published his fourth book, *The Universal Constant in Living*, and then returned to England.

In 1947 Alexander suffered a severe stroke following a bad fall. He was seventy-nine and the prognosis was unhopeful. But by the March of the following year he was back at work and he continued teaching until he died on 10 October 1955 in his eighty-seventh year.

Alexander's achievements and the technique which he taught

found many influential apologists, including G. B. Shaw, Aldous Huxley, Sir Stafford Cripps and William Temple, Archbishop of Canterbury. He also had many enthusiastic supporters in the medical profession – though too few to effect the practical follow-through either in prophylactic or curative medicine which his work deserved; also the establishment and continuity of his work was badly interrupted by the war when many of his trainee teachers were called up. Now the picture is better. There are many fully trained teachers and the Alexander Technique is taught and practised in many countries. Its use in Britain and the USA in the training of actors, musicians and singers has long been widespread and continues to grow.

Alexander's discovery that 'use determines function' and his evolution of a technique which enables the use of the body to be re-educated and freed from unhelpful or damaging habitual patterns of response remains, in my view, one of the potentially most important innovations which our culture has produced.

Names and addresses of those properly qualified to teach the Alexander Technique will be supplied upon request and the supply of a stamped addressed envelope by The Secretary, Society of Teachers of the Alexander Technique, 10 London House, 266 Fulham Road, London SW10 9EL. In the USA information may be obtained from The American Centre for the Alexander Technique Inc., 142 West End Avenue, New York, NY 10023.

Select Bibliography

———

This is a short list of books and pamphlets culled from the many consulted during the writing of *The Voice Book*. Some of them I have found useful in my own teaching practice and work as a director, and some of them are, as well, the standard works of reference in their particular fields. I include a brief personal appraisal of each work listed. Some of the books are out of print and may only be easily obtainable from libraries. Publications marked * are only available direct from the publishers.

Body use

Alexander, F. Matthias, *The Use of Self*, New York, Dutton, 1932; paperback, Long Beach, California, Centerline Press, 1984
The clearest exposition by Alexander of the evolution of his technique.

Man's Supreme Inheritance, London and New York, Dutton, 1941; paperback, Long Beach, California, Centerline Press, 1987

Constructive Conscious Control of the Individual, London, Methuen, 1924; New York, Dutton, 1923; paperback with new introduction by W. H. M. Carrington, Long Beach, California, Centerline Press, 1985

The Universal Constant in Living, New York, Dutton, 1941; paperback with new introduction by Patrick Macdonald, Long Beach, California, Centerline Press, 1986
Alexander's own books are the original written sources of description and analysis of the technique which he discovered and which he constantly evolved during his long practice as a teacher; but the practical work of his own assistants and the teachers they have trained offer, in my view, a much better introduction to the technique than any of the books. The books reveal themselves best to those who have some practical experience of the work.

Barlow, Wilfred, *The Alexander Principle*, London, Gollancz, 1973; also in paperback
A doctor, one of Alexander's pupils, reassesses the technique and the benefits it offers for improved general health; interesting illustrations.

Carrington, W. H. M., *Balance as a Function of Intelligence,** London, The Sheildrake Press, 1974
The author was Alexander's assistant during a vital period in the development of the technique. A good introductory pamphlet.

Gelb, Michael, *Body Learning*, London, Aurum Press, 1981; New York, Henry Holt, 1981
An introduction to the Alexander Technique with many excellent illustrations.

Jones, Frank Pierce, *Learning How to Learn,** London, The Sheildrake Press, 1974
This is a pamphlet by the distinguished American philosopher and educator on the Alexander Technique as an aid to the whole process of learning.

Body Awareness in Action, New York, Schocken Books, 1976
The implications of the Alexander Technique re-examined. Not an easy read but worth the trouble, particularly when the reader has some experience of the technique.

Speech

Abercrombie, David, *Elements of General Phonetics*, Edinburgh University Press, 1967
Good on the syllable.

Gimson, A. C., *An Introduction to the Pronunciation of English* (Third Edition), London, Edward Arnold, 1980
The standard work on the subject; clear, mostly easy to read and thorough.

Jones, Daniel, *Everyman's English Pronouncing Dictionary* (Fourteenth Edition revised by A. C. Gimson), London, Dent, 1977. New York, Dutton
This is the best guide to current Standard English pronunciation and is updated every few years.

Muirden, Ronald, *Stammering Correction Simplified*, London, J. Garnett Miller, 1971
In some cases of stammering Mr Muirden's approach would probably prove oversimplified, but it's still the most practically helpful book I know dealing with this problem.

Pichon, E., and Borel-Maisonny, S., *Le Bégaiement (Sa Nature et Son Traitement)* (Third Edition), Paris, Masson, 1979
I am unable to find an English translation of this illuminating work on the nature of stammering; a thorough exposition of the subject, cause and effect; conclusions as to treatment are more arguable.

Kenyon, John S., and Knott, Thomas A., *A Pronouncing Dictionary of American English*, Springfield, Mass., USA, Merriam-Webster Inc., Publishers, 1953.

Breathing and tuning

Denes, Peter B. and Pinson, Elliot N., *The Speech Chain*, USA, Bell
    Telephone Laboratories, 1972
The physics of sound carefully explained and related to the voice.

Husler, Frederick, and Rodd-Marling, Yvonne, *Singing – the Physical
    Nature of the Vocal Organ* (Revised Edition), London, Hutchinson,
    1976
More of a teacher's book perhaps than for the general student. A very clear exposition
of the functioning of the voice in singing, extremely well illustrated. This book has
provoked controversy in the singing world but I've yet to encounter a convincing
rebuttal of its arguments.

Husson, Raoul, *Le Chant*, Paris, Presses Universitaires de France, 1962;
    no English edition available
A detailed look at the functioning of the vocal cords and vocal registers in singing.

Vennard, William, *Singing: The Mechanism and the Technic*, New York,
    Carl Fischer, 1967
A massive tome full of well-explained knowledge about the functioning of the
singing voice with an idiosyncratic view of what makes for good sound. Impressive
illustrations, including sequences of photographs of the vocal cords in action.

General

Laban, Rudolf, and Lawrence, F. C., *Effort* (Second Edition), Plymouth,
    Macdonald and Evans, 1974; paperback

Laban, Rudolf, *The Mastery of Movement*, Plymouth, Macdonald and
    Evans, 1963
These two books give Laban's analysis of the dynamics of movement – a help
towards understanding the basis of many of the developments in the teaching of
movement in the theatre during the last fifty years.

Barker, Clive, *Theatre Games*, London, Eyre-Methuen, 1977; paperback
Good 'change' exercises; an important book in the evolution of the teaching of basic
acting skills; excellent for company work.

Gorman, David, *The Body Moveable*,* Ontario, Ampersand Press, 1985
An anatomical atlas which brilliantly clarifies the relation between skeleton and
muscle in the moving body; by far the most comprehensible book of its kind that
I've seen.

Punt, Norman A., *The Singer's and Actor's Throat* (Third Edition, London,
    Heinemann, 1979
All about 'the mechanism of the professional voice user and its care in health and
disease'.

Index

Fluffed lines, in radio work,
205–6; in dubbing work, 210
Fog-horn voice, 86
Fricative [ɹ], 161–3

Games, in warm-ups, 213
Gasping, 5, 9, 15, 42–4, in
breathy voice, 81
Gesture, voice an extension of,
182–4
'Getting the feel of the part', 197
Glide exercise, 95
Glottic attack or shock, 41, 85
Glottis, 12, 36, 61, 83; breath
pressure at, 36, 38; glottic
popping, 83–5

Habitual response, need to
overcome, 4, 7–9, 14–15, 20–2
Hard palate, 78–9, 117;
vibrations in, 89; *see also*
Alveolar ridge
Head cold, 217–18; effect on
resonance, 71, 86; simulation as
test of nasality, 88
Head/neck/back relationship, 6, 9,
12, 15–17, 22; in exercises, 25,
27, 48; in everyday life, 28; in
stage fright, 32; loss in fatigue,
36; in support, 37, 39;
associated with nodules, 82; in
register problems, 95; in trying
to fill space, 103–4; in undoing
rehearsal blocks, 198–200; in
pre-performance warm-up,
211–12
Head voice or register, 78;
immaturity in isolated use, 93;
inability to use, 97; *see also*
Registers

High notes, 9, 79, 91, 100–1;
prevented by pulling down, 97;
open mouth/throat in, 99;
resonance of, 103; tendency to
be too loud, 108–9
Hip joint, 18, 28
Humidity, need for, 215
Humming, 74–5; for nasal
resonance, 90
Hump back, *see* Richard III
Husky voice, 80
Hysterics, acting without strain,
101; breathing in, 225

Imagery and imagination, use of
in voice work, 80, 104–5, 185;
in changing body use, 184, 186;
in role development, 188–9,
198
Imitation in voice use, 101–2; of
the band and the zoo, 107; of
other people, 107–8, 188–92
Inhibition, 129–30, *see also*
Shyness
Interpretation (of role), *see also*
Characterization;
predetermined, 186–9
Intimate scene, voice quality in,
104
Intrusive 'r', 162
Irish accent, [ł] in, 163
Irregular breathing pattern,
14–15

Jaw, common misuses, 9, 15; free
in clear speech, 124–5, 139; in
making consonants, 144–6;
dissociated from lips, 141–2;
release in 'stopping', 22, for
pipe smokers, 216, in exercises